The Problematic Fictions of Poe, James, and Hawthorne

The Problematic Fictions of Poe, James, and Hawthorne

Judith L. Sutherland

University of Missouri Press
Columbia, 1984

University of Missouri Press, Columbia, Missouri 65211
Printed and bound in the United States of America

Library of Congress Cataloging in Publication Data

Sutherland, Judith L.
The problematic fictions of Poe, James, and Hawthorne.

Bibliography: p.
Includes index.
1. American fiction—19th century—History and criticism. 2. Poe, Edgar Allan, 1809–1849. Narrative of Arthur Gordon Pym. 3. Hawthorne, Nathaniel, 1804–1864. Marble faun. 4. James, Henry, 1843–1916. Sacred fount. I. Title.
PS377.S97 1984 813'.3'09 83-16817
ISBN 0-8262-0434-1

To Howard Laster

Preface

The method of inquiry used in this book arose in part from my dissatisfaction with thematic criticism, from a sense that the explication of themes fails to provide the critical reader with an experience of the movement of the text. More important, it arose out of the novels themselves. Each of these works seemed still to call for a new way of reading in order to meet what Jonathan Culler has described as "the fundamental demand of the system: the demand for sense" (*Structuralist Poetics,* London: Routledge and Kegan Paul, 1975). In addition to Culler's works, three others have had an important bearing on my own work: Charles Feidelson's *Symbolism and American Literature,* John F. Lynen's *The Design of the Present,* and Tony Tanner's *City of Words.*

This book began as a dissertation at the University of Iowa, written with the support of an Educational Foundation Fellowship from the American Association of University Women. My first thanks, then and now, are to my teacher Sherman Paul. He offers critical dialogue at its best, and I have been the beneficiary. I would also like to thank Alfred Kazin for our discussions of Poe during the summer of 1976, when he was a visiting professor at Iowa. Donald Marshall and Robert Scharlemann read the manuscript at crucial stages and provided helpful advice. Howard Laster, Dean of the College of Liberal Arts at the University of Iowa, to whom this book is dedicated, has been a constant source of encouragement. My final thanks are to my husband, Donald W. Sutherland, who was with me at every step of the way and who did all those things and more for which spouses are thanked in prefaces.

Contents

The sense of an unnatural symbolism always settled back on him again. Each figure seemed to be, somehow, on the borderland of things, just as their theory was on the borderland of thought. He knew that each of these men stood at the extreme end, so to speak, of some wild road of reasoning. He could only fancy, as in some old-world fable, that if a man went westward to the end of the world he would find something—say a tree—that was more or less than a tree, a tree possessed by a spirit; and that if he went east to the end of the world he would find something else that was not wholly itself—a tower, perhaps, of which the very shape was wicked. So these figures seemed to stand up, violent and unaccountable, against an ultimate horizon, visions from the verge. The ends of the earth were closing in.

—G. K. Chesterton, *The Man Who Was Thursday*

Introduction

Several distinct but related concerns prompted the studies that make up this book. The texts chosen, Edgar Poe's *Narrative of Arthur Gordon Pym,* Henry James's *Sacred Fount,* and Nathaniel Hawthorne's *Marble Faun,* though offering no simple solutions and, in fact, externally offering no resolutions at all, did promise to sharpen the definitions of the problems that concerned me. Individually, each text is a version of the hermeneutical nightmare. Taken together, they address the issues and reveal the inadequacies of whatever critical stances we choose to assume toward the texts that make up the American symbolist tradition.

These three works bring a special pressure to bear on the fallacy of thematic interpretation because they are capable of generating an endless number of themes. To borrow a Jamesian term, we are invited to pick up a thread and follow it through to the end. Each theme seems capable of imposing coherence up to a point, but it is then undercut by the text. The chosen theme may be more or less abstract. If narrowly particular, it does not ring true or illuminate the work for others because it seems too much a function of the special framework that the critic uses to comprehend American literature. A good example of this phenomenon is seen in the discovery of psychological themes in Poe. Incest, necrophilia, compulsion, each has had its day as the single, underlying theme running through all his work. Yet if we try to sidestep this difficulty by generalizing the theme, looking for an overriding theme that will encompass the lesser ones, we compromise the particularity of individual works and of individual authors.

The texts studied here undermine so obviously any thematic approach that the only alternative seems to be to adopt a more formal stance, one that allows us to explore the appeal made and "the special nature of our responses to it."[1] In other words, our attention must be focused on the rhetorical relationship established by the text. Critical inquiry becomes a record of the way the text manipulates its reader.

Unfortunately, this alternative carries with it a new set of difficulties. When we treat the text in this way, the surface story is robbed of its importance. Pushed far enough, this approach produces a peculiarly bloodless kind of criticism. It has led Kenneth Dauber to assert, "Hawthorne's works are structures that contain no vision. From the point of view of his purpose they are forms without subjects."[2]

When attention is focused on formal method rather than on subject matter, the text becomes a point of departure for one more epistemological theory. Emersonian aesthetics emphasized and encouraged this shift in attention from matter to method, but Emerson warned that the tendency to plunge the thinker into abstraction must be kept in check by keeping a hold on the natural facts. Poe's *Pym*, however, reveals that the gulf between the natural facts of the text and the aesthetic experience created by its formal structure is so wide that any link between the two extremes becomes virtually impossible. Like Pynchon's heroine, Oedipa Maas, in *The Crying of Lot 49*, the critic is faced with the choice of being left with "compiled memories, announcements, intimations" that have no real coherence or with a central truth "too bright for memory to hold." The aesthetic experience created in *Pym* seeks to evade language. It reveals with a vengeance the inability of critical discourse to seize and record that experience. This is equally true of our other two texts; all reveal gaps between the surface story or referential aspects of the language and the formal structure created by the language.

In *City of Words*, Tony Tanner introduces the term *foregrounding*, which is very close to the preoccupation with form that I am describing. Fiction that is highly foregrounded uses language in a way that draws attention to the language itself. In other words, the aesthetic experience of such works is shifted to the formal patterns created (and destroyed) and to their effect upon the reader. Most relevant to our discussion is Tanner's assertion that behind this process lies "a general self-consciousness about the strange relationship between the provinces of words and things, and the problematical position of man, who participates in both."[3]

The issues raised here are commonplace in the experience of the reader of contemporary American literature, which often partakes of indeterminacy and self-reflexiveness. Charles Feidelson's distinctive *Symbolism and American Literature* explores their emergence in the struggles of the writers of the American Renaissance with a symbolist aesthetic. Feidelson's work, however, places Melville at the center of that tradition, claiming that Hawthorne and Poe are somehow then "off-center." From a certain point of view Hawthorne and Poe (and James too) are off-center; they approach the whole symbolist enterprise with a skepticism that Melville evidenced only in his later writings. Feidelson writes of Melville, "Pursuing the symbolic voyage to the utmost, but realizing at the same time its ineffectuality, Ahab is ruined and Melville discovers that he is potentially an Ahab, the devil's partisan, the nihilist. Poe begins where Ahab leaves off."[4] Hawthorne, as we shall see, was anxious not to repeat Poe, while James had the benefit of both Poe's and Hawthorne's insights.

These three writers represent a conservative stance in regard to Emerson's blurring of the lines between words and things, literature and life. Like T. E. Hulme and T. S. Eliot after them, they approached the problem with a clear understanding of the moral implications it involves. When they postulated an art of a fluid and inconclusive nature, to paraphrase Feidelson's charge against Eliot, they did so with the knowledge that the literature they produced smacks of the heretical. I have no objection to their being viewed as off-center for refusing to embrace the symbolist aesthetic with Melville's enthusiasm. To imply, however, that their more conservative stance prevented them from coming fully to terms with it is inaccurate. The three works I have chosen to study here represent each author's explicit confrontation with the symbolic mode. Although these problematic works may or may not "save symbolism," they do illustrate "all that can be said for and against the symbolic method."[5]

The role of displacement and the nature of analogy form the nucleus of the issues raised. The two in conjunction allow us to understand why the American approach to poetics is so often termed "oddly religious."[6] Here I use the term *displacement* in the sense that Northop Frye employs in *The Anatomy of Criticism.* Myth, according to Frye, is the realm of implicit metaphorical identity; realism, the realm of implicit simile. Romance is defined as a tendency "to displace myth in a human direction and yet, in contrast to 'realism,' to conventionalize content in an idealized direction."[7] Moreover, "The central principle of displacement is that what can be metaphorically identified in a myth can only be linked in romance by some form of simile: analogy, significant association, incidental accompanying imagery, and the like."

The problem is that we are never sure just what degree of likeness resides in analogy as it is used by our writers or what constitutes a significant association (Frye's context implies a connotation of self-consciousness or intentionality). Nor is it at all clear that our writers themselves are certain of where the boundaries lie. Myth and private dream are two realms where metaphorical identity operates; the three novels I examine push at both boundaries. The nameless narrator of James's work alternately sees his vision as having the inclusiveness of the grand scheme of myth or as being no more than a private nightmare imposed on the world around him. Similarly, Hawthorne's vision is portrayed as both an all-compassing structure and a tiny jeweled casket. The objections to thematic criticism mentioned above are reflected and echoed here. Writ small, such criticism conveys a private dream; writ large it verges on myth and loses touch with the text. As a method, it only recapitulates the problems presented by American texts and does not resolve them.

Although the problem of the nature of analogy has been present in American literature from the first, it is accentuated when outside referents disappear. John F. Lynen has pointed out that Puritan poems reveal a commitment to a new form of poetry in which analogy is the dominant mode.[8] But a check is placed on the use of analogy in Puritan poetics. For the Puritan poet, analogy was always a form of likeness and not one of identity. His work remains free of the ambiguity that emerges in later American writing, an ambiguity that arises in part because we are never sure whether comparison is merely comparison or whether it is meant to suggest metaphorical identity.

The problem raises both aesthetic and moral questions because moral attitudes define the aesthetic possibilities open to the artist. Discussing Edward Taylor's poetic merit, Lynen says that Taylor's failings are attributable to his attitudes rather than to his skill: "Something in Taylor's mind acts as an impediment to metaphysical poetry, forcing him to hold back, as it were. He cannot fully exploit the conceit, because however elaborately developed, it remains for him an analogy."[9] What held Taylor back was the orthodox Christian tradition of which he was a part; it posited an essential difference between the present and the eternal aspects of reality, between the physical and spiritual world, between man's nature and God's.

Emerson's great innovation some one hundred years later was removing the impediment that had kept earlier writers, such as Taylor and Anne Bradstreet, from fully exploiting the conceit. Like the Puritan poets, he also realized that man's attitudes toward language reflect his attitude toward the relationship between man and God. Emerson sought to eliminate the differences between nature (which includes human nature) and the spiritual. Nature is a source of direct revelation; the word is the thing. His new aesthetics opened up a realm of apparently unrestricted freedom for the American artist. It also opened a Pandora's box. The American artist has since been hard pressed to discover how to exploit the advantages of Emersonian aesthetics while at the same time maintaining a position that keeps him free of its theological implications. The refusal to accept Emerson's flirtation with the idea of man's close identity to God underlies what Tony Tanner has called the American writer's "radical distrust of language." Tanner points out that "American writers evince a heightened awareness of the separateness of words and things," that "there has been from the start in American literature an intermittent sense of the futility of pretending that the putative exactitude of words can ever measure up to the actual mystery of things. Along with this has gone a suspicion that there can be something damaging in confusing names and their referents."[10] Speaking of the same sort of paradoxical attitude that I have mentioned above, Tanner adds, "There is a detectable element of radical distrust of language among many American writers, even while paradoxically they must perforce continue to work with it to preserve the extended range of mental possibilities it makes available."

After Emerson, it has rested with individual American authors to define their attitude toward this problem. *Pym, The Sacred Fount*, and *The Marble Faun* are such definitive fictions. I begin with the *Narrative of Arthur Gordon Pym* and *The Sacred Fount* because, despite their similarities, they provide us with two polarities of response. The two books share the distinction of being superb failures. Both sold less well than any other work of Poe or James, respectively. Roundly rejected by the reading public, they shared a similar fate at the hands of their authors. Poe's one reference to *Pym* passes it off as too extravagant, a silly book. James was even more vehement in his rejection of *The Sacred Fount*.

Both "failures" were experiments in the use of a first-person narrator who proves to be unreliable. James employed the first person in only a few of his short stories and in none of his other novels. Though Poe used the first person more often, *Pym* is his only attempt in the novel form. More interesting is the fact that these experimental failures appeared in the midst of or just prior to some highly successful writing by both authors. *Pym*, written sometime before June 1837, shares the stage with some of Poe's greatest stories: "Ligeia," "William Wilson," and "The Fall of the House of Usher." *The Sacred Fount* was immediately followed by *The Ambassadors*, and it has been argued that it served as a kind of trial run for the latter. The chronological position of these two novels thus reinforces the idea that they are experiments, that they may have been used to clarify or resolve problems whose solutions cleared the ground for the successes that followed.

It is more difficult to designate any one particular work of Hawthorne's as problematical. One could argue that the obvious choice is *The Blithedale Romance.* With its elusive first-person narrator it bears a clear resemblance to *Pym* and *The Sacred Fount.* It stands between the turning toward and the turning away from the symbolist aesthetic of Poe and James because it represents the same confrontation yet provides no resolution. In it, as Richard Brodhead states, Hawthorne reached "an impasse both in his formal practice and in his sense of life."[11] But to choose *Blithedale* would have led to a far different kind of inquiry. The focus of this work would have been on James and his resolution of the problem in the later novels. This book is about Hawthorne and his attempt at a resolution in his last complete novel, *The Marble Faun.* And although *The Marble Faun* carries the problem a step beyond *Pym* and *The Sacred Fount,* it still shares many of the same characteristics. All three texts hover on the borderline between romance and an absurd self-parody, employing forms that force romantic premises to the breaking point. From this vantage point they show us both what is gained by the freedom provided by an analogy of identification and educate us to its dangers. We begin to see why American writers have felt the need to incorporate checks and balances on the extended range of mental possibilities offered them in Emerson's aesthetic. For as these works illustrate, an unchecked analogy leads to nihilism and the absurd.

Poe recognized that Emerson's injunction to hold to the natural fact had no sanction other than that of a gentleman's agreement, and Poe, a sporadic gentleman at best, was quick to abandon it. Letting go, he was able to explore an aesthetics of the absurd and reap the advantages it offered. Nevertheless, he was canny enough to impose his own check upon it by limiting the length of his stories (to the time needed to produce a single effect) and thus prevent a blatant exposure of the negative features that were inherent in it. His audience experiences the full brunt of this aesthetic only in *Pym,* his one extended fiction.

Much later Henry James was to repeat the experiment. His particular way into the absurd, or what he was to call "the high fantastic," is through the use of a first-person narrator whose unchecked egotism is allowed to shape and misshape the reality around him at will. James often spoke cavalierly of the book in later years, but there is also ample evidence that he found this particular literary experiment unsettling and its implications disturbing. It did allow him to catch a glimpse of what lay ahead in cubism, and Gertrude Stein may well have had this particular work in mind when she spoke of James as pointing the way to her own experimental fictions.

What was the effect of this experiment on James's later work? On the one hand, he embraced the new freedom he discovered and became even more concerned with form. Or as Arnold P. Hinchcliffe claims, he "adopted a more American mode of writing akin to the romances of Hawthorne and Melville."[12] And American it proved to be. Given a new freedom, James also showed an increased concern for placing new boundaries, new checks and balances upon his fiction. His later novels are presented through a narrative voice that is carefully qualified in its freedom by screens and filters. His subject matter, too, is winnowed and refined to exclude more and more elements. This tendency to impose limitations and qualifications has always been associated with Hawthorne, but it is equally present in James's fiction. Even a brief survey of the standard critical works presents an array of titles (*The Crystal Cage, The Expense of Vision, The Negative Imagination*) that point to a check on the freedom of the imagination, to a weighing of the cost of a given aesthetic.

All this is reminiscent of Hawthorne's injunction to keep the imagination sane. James did have Hawthorne's tragedy, his failure to preserve the sanity of the imaginative realm, always before him. Any student of the two soon realizes how much of James's work recapitulates Hawthorne's, how James reworked his predecessor's themes and sought to recast and resolve the problems that defeated Hawthorne. For Hawthorne represents the classic case of the American author caught between the new formal freedom offered by the American romantic aesthetic and the need to limit it.

Hawthorne seems always to have been more or less aware of the threat that an uncontrolled analogy held for his writing. In the quotation from "P.'s Correspondence" with which I begin the discussion of *The Marble Faun,* he rejects P.'s "misty excursions beyond the limits of sanity." "Correspondence" is both P.'s letters that make up much of the story and the transcendental idea of correspondence. Poe and his use of the absurd were what Hawthorne had in mind here. The narrative voice dismisses such "misty excursions" with a kind of easy condescension. Hawthorne himself did not escape so easily. He felt a constant pressure at his back to move his fictions toward the absurd. Poe, very early, caught this note of strain in Hawthorne's work. In the 1847 essay "Tale Writing: Nathaniel Hawthorne," he warned Hawthorne to beware of "metaphor run mad," which Poe found even then damaging Hawthorne's fictions.[13] He advised him to avoid the snares of mysticism and to reject the whole transcendental milieu by turning to a more realistic vein. Both Poe's and Hawthorne's term for this is *sunshine,* and Hawthorne's desire to write a "sunshiny" novel as well as his endless efforts to incorporate some element of realism into his tales are too well known to require further comment here. Suffice it to say that he was able to maintain the balance of romance and realism that he believed his work required—until he undertook the writing of *The Marble Faun.*

In *The Faun,* correspondence runs amuck. While struggling "to preserve the extended range of mental possibilities" that correspondence provides, Hawthorne virtually strangled his text with checks and balances aimed at countering the book's spiritual implications. Despite his efforts, the gap between the surface meaning and the realities Hawthorne would direct his reader toward becomes so great that the work is tinged throughout with an air of absurdity and nihilism. The recurring image of the Laocoön is often cited for its pathos and power. Much of its effect must come from its being not only an image of man caught in the coils of error and evil but from its representation of the artist inextricably caught in the coils of his own mental and spiritual reservations. By the time Hawthorne undertook *The Dolliver Romance,* the last of the unfinished novels, the balance that kept his romances on the edge of absurdity had dissolved. As he confessed to his friend and publisher, James Fields, "Seriously, my mind has, for the present, lost its temper and its fine edge, and I have an instinct that I had better keep quiet."[14]

Behind this concern to place limits is an effort to avoid Emerson's too facile identification of object and idea, of man and God. Exploring the limits of analogy is one way of exploring the boundary lines between morality and art. In the rhetorical relationships presented in these works, the question of identity between man and God emerges as a consideration of how far the artist's role of creator is like God's role. Poe, though he always remains elusive in respect to the problem, came closest to proposing a metaphorical identity. God is an artist whose plots are perfect. Conversely, the artist plays a God-like role in relation to his reader. As Poe stated in a review of *Twice-Told Tales,* "During the hour of perusal the soul of the reader is at the writer's control."[15]

Benefiting from his distance in both time and place from Poe, James could see clearly the kinds of concessions that the text must suffer in order for the artist to maintain this position. His respect for the inviolate nature of both his characters and readers seems to stand in the way of his adopting such a willful aesthetic. One of his characters summarizes his final assessment of the situation when she tells the narrator-artist of *The Sacred Fount* (who is busy constructing "scenes" and "plots"), "You can't be a *providence,* and not be a bore."[16]

Hawthorne's position is less easy to state in such succinct terms. As so often happens in trying to interpret his stance, the critic struggles for a precarious balance that no matter how formally awkward will somehow convey the truth of the matter. One can simply say that Hawthorne was a traditionalist, a conservative. For him there was no question of the artist being God-like. At best, he posited the artist as a redeemer figure and art itself as playing a redeeming role in human life. In *The Marble Faun,* Dante and Milton are held up as exemplars, artists whose works can spiritually enlighten a reader and comfort him in times of trial. But in that book, art, like everything else, is fallen. The artist can no longer produce a *Divine Comedy* or *Paradise Lost*. The only role left to him is that of a negative redeemer. Like Kierkegaard's "corrective," he is reduced to pointing out what has gone awry, to helping his audience understand the conditions that make it impossible to create an art that is heroic or consecrated as in the old style.

Nevertheless, an ambivalence lurks in Hawthorne's seeming humility. While he declared that art has lost its power for good, his every gesture asserts that it has not lost its power for evil. Unlike James, he never really trusted his audience. His abiding fear was that his aesthetic would lead the reader to a vision of nihilism without providing the means of moving beyond that dark vision. Consequently, Hawthorne was forced again and again to hedge in his naive reader protectively and, in doing so, to undermine the powerful thrust of his own fictions. In the modern works that have done much to generate a reader-response approach, the powers and limitations of consciousness in the act of imposing meaning become a matter of critical debate. The texts I have chosen carry that debate to extreme lengths. The reader is invited to render judgments, to find a position from which he can view dispassionately the rhetorical appeals made by these fictions. Yet while urging judgment, the texts repeatedly thwart it by undermining the reader's relationship to the text and destroying the distance needed. The reader discovers that positions promising to allow him to step outside the text lead to a labyrinth of unlimited abstract speculation or into the equally fantastic realm of a subtle solipsism.

Pym, *The Sacred Fount*, and *The Marble Faun* educate the reader to the dangers of subjectivity that are inherent in the reader-response approach. To put it more positively, they teach us a healthy respect for their "otherness," for their own integrity. We are invited to play the role of Dupin ever mindful that we will not, nor are we intended to, emerge as a victorious Dupin. With that warning let us turn to the harshest of our three taskmasters, Edgar Allan Poe.

I. Poe: The Captain Regrets . . .

> The only sin is limitation.
>
> —Ralph Waldo Emerson, "Circles"

> With as deep a reverence for the True that ever inspired the bosom of man, I would, nevertheless, limit, in some measure, its modes of inculcation. I would limit to enforce them.
>
> —Edgar Allan Poe, "The Poetic Principle"

With the exception of Emerson, there is perhaps no figure in American literature so protean as Edgar Poe. Toward both men we feel a deep ambivalence. Yet the ambivalence felt toward Poe is harsher and more radical than that felt toward Emerson. We know that Emerson is a "man without a handle." We cannot assert even this with any finality about Poe. That we cannot is in itself a basic part of the "Poe game" that each new generation of critics is seduced into playing with our most elusive author. In every new encounter with Poe's work, the critical reader is led to believe that the handle, the key to Poe, lies just below the surface and that with a little more effort, though his critical faculties are already at the breaking point, it will be revealed. In fact, there is no key, but a handle is offered us in that we are endlessly invited to hope for such a key though continually thwarted in our efforts to find it.

Poe's texts afford us so much difficulty because they create rhetorical situations in which it is nearly impossible to discover a "safe" critical position. Critical responses are anticipated by the text and thus are an integral part of it. This difficulty is mirrored in the various stances taken by critics of Poe's work.

Probably more than any other major American writer, Poe

has been the subject of what might be called an oblique or glancing criticism. His sources have been carefully traced. His life and work have been subjected to close psychoanalytical scrutiny. These methods, however, allow the critic to maintain a certain strict distance from the actual text. The text is engaged obliquely. At the opposite extreme stands Baudelaire, an admirer who gladly immersed himself in Poe's texts and translated them. Despite his enthusiasm, he too seems to have sensed the dangers of the middle ground of criticism and avoided them, urging his contemporary, St. Beuve, to undertake that task.[1]

What is it that makes so sacrosanct this area between? Why is it that if one loves Poe's work or is even enough convinced of his genius to be an admirer, one feels that somehow the land of encounter with the text itself is a no-man's-land? Why does one emerge from it not like some Ancient Mariner primed to speak compulsively but under a ban of silence? The Mariner emerges from his experience chastised but not nearly so chastised as Poe's reader. The Mariner still believes in the efficacy of language. The reader of Poe has come to doubt even that.[2]

There is some justification in critical readings that attempt to hold Poe at more than arm's length. It may be no more than the simple wisdom of "he who sups with the devil must use a long spoon." More than one critic has called Poe's aesthetic diabolic. Diabolic or not, the aesthetic he employed serves to dictate to a greater degree than most writers the kind of critical response that can be made to the work. Again, the possible responses seem to divide into two concerns that in many ways appear to be irreconcilable.

The first response is that already touched upon: the long, cool view. Here Poe's writings are treated seriously. Symbols are carefully explicated and their integration into thematic patterns is often convincingly illustrated. But once one has arrived at the theme—necrophilia, obsession, incest, and so on—one feels somehow oddly cheated. Such critical treatment seems far too static to account for the experience of reading Poe. G. R. Thompson expresses his dissatisfaction with this kind of reading by saying that it treats a Poe story as a single phenomenon and fails to relate it to the whole of

Poe's work.[3] The insulated quality of such responses goes much deeper.

The more complete experience of Poe that Thompson is arguing for *can* be gotten by extending the number of texts considered, yet there is no guarantee that a more complete reading will result. The elements that are wanting are usually contained in any single Poe story. The problem is that the imposition of any kind of structure is invited by the text. The invitation and our response to it form the basis of the rhetorical transaction. What is ignored is the way that the text simultaneously undermines the structuring activity that it has invited. The picture remains incomplete because the first part of this transaction, the imposition of a structure, is faithfully recorded; the second part, the destructive side, is ignored.

A covert acknowledgment of the danger and hostility that threaten the reader of Poe's fiction is at least partly responsible for the recent critical popularity of "The House of Usher," "Ligeia," and "William Wilson." Their mechanics make them accessible to the critic while at the same time affording him immunity. Each story involves a narrator who is intimately involved with a second figure. The intimacy of that involvement is a matter of degree, from the less to the greater in the order that the stories are listed above. Critical discussion can focus primarily on the involvement of the narrator with the figure that fills his landscape. It allows the critic to neglect or obscure the further relationship of *reader* to narrator to central figure.

It is precisely in this area of the reader's response that critical discourse breaks down. If the critical reader rejects thematic criticism and attempts to engage the text more directly, the most likely alternative would seem to be an attempt to confront Poe's language. Yet this confrontation creates more problems than it solves. The writer finds himself immersed in an enterprise that appears, even to him, unsavory.[4] In an introductory essay to *The Narrative of Arthur Gordon Pym*, Richard Wilbur briefly indulges in this kind of response:

> One's sense of this kind of content in Pym begins with the hero's name: "Arthur Gordon Pym" has the same number and disposition of syllables as "Edgar Allan Poe," the same

> terminal *r* and *n,* the same initial *P.* The fourth sentence of the story proper refers to Pym's grandfather's holdings in "the Edgarton New Bank," and soon thereafter we are told that Pym, as a boy, studied under "old Mr. Ricketts, a gentleman with only one arm." According to J. H. Whitty, there was in fact a one-armed schoolmaster of that name in Poe's home city of Richmond. There is no report—to proceed with the names in Pym's first paragraph—of a Richmond schoolmaster named "E. Ronald," yet the reader may be forgiven, after so much nameplay, if he notes that "Ronald" is an anagram of "Arnold," the family name of Poe's mother Elizabeth. The name of Pym's school-friend, Augustus Bernard, is less obviously suggestive, since recent biography has made little mention of Poe's boyhood companion, Ebenezer Burling. But it will readily be seen that "Augustus" and "Ebenezer" have eight letters each, while Barnard and Burling have seven each and initial "B" in common.[5]

The question here is not whether these observations are true. I am quite inclined to accept them as both true and valid. The list can even be added to, not perhaps in terms of autobiographical detail but certainly in terms of the wordplay in the first page of the story proper. There is an interesting alliterative play at the end of the third sentence in which *A*rthur Gordon *P*ym's maternal grandfather is introduced as an "*a*ttorney in *g*ood *p*ractice." There is an odd coincidence in the choice of New Bedford as a city name in the same paragraph that reveals that Arthur and Augustus share the same bed. There is a similarly odd coincidence in Pym's boat being called the *Ariel:* the storm that destroys it is several times referred to in the next few pages as a "tempest."

It might be objected that there is a definitive difference between Wilbur's examples and these I propose. All of Wilbur's examples form a kind of connection among themselves; they all involve nameplay rather than mere wordplay. All have in common that they are autobiographical. My examples, on the other hand, allow the mind no room for extension, for generalization, from the facts. They are trivial in that there are no connections among them, and they lead nowhere. If they are to be enjoyed, they can only be enjoyed on a very low level, in and for themselves.

I would answer that the difference is only one of degree. Autobiographical "facts" do appear at the beginning of *Pym*, but as Wilbur concedes, "It must be granted that, once the story gets under way, the autobiographical touches grow rare, and that it is vain to look for parallels between Pym's adventures and the literal career of Edgar Poe." Wilbur's observations have the advantage that they can to some extent be structured; mine cannot. Still, the two sets of observations share an important element—they lead nowhere.

As critical readers, both Wilbur and I feel apologetic in leading our readers into this kind of pursuit. Tracking down puns seems trivial because they offer, by their very nature, an ephemeral and isolated pleasure. Yet it is this same insular quality that pervades the thematic criticism applied to Poe's works and makes the thematic approach unsatisfactory. Like the pun, the themes of incest, obsession, and compulsion have an intrinsic interest. Nevertheless, though capable of producing horror and revulsion, they do not account for these elements in Poe's fiction. To cite one instance, the incest theme in *Oedipus* evokes a horror that has nothing in it of the horror of Poe's work.

I noted earlier the tendency of critics to avoid a direct encounter with Poe, to treat him obliquely. I have also tried to illustrate how a direct encounter with the language leaves one feeling slightly ridiculous. Thematic criticism is a larger model of the same process. The thematic structure is larger and more complete, but it is unsatisfactory because it fails to touch the sources of fear and anxiety that Poe's work arouses even in sophisticated readers. We find ourselves in the same position that Patrick Quinn ascribes to Baudelaire, who, "no matter how intense his emotional response to this work, could not readily communicate the secret of his feelings about it."[6]

I believe the real horror in Poe lies in his having successfully employed language to create a hermeneutical nightmare. As soon as we assent to enter Poe's world, we are invited to ask questions. Every work of art offers that kind of invitation, presenting its questions to us as part of the communication. But in Poe's world the questions lack the innocence of simple invitation. It is a spider-fly world: behind the invitation lurks the force of seduction. And the seduction has no end. Every question asked leads to frustration. Every structured answer we impose on a Poe story betrays other elements in the story that are capable of effectively undermining that structure. Part of the horror derives from this rhythmical construction and collapse of our mental structures.

But there is another source of horror. We find ourselves horrified at our own reactions to the situation. Once involved in this world, we discover that our response to this frustration is not to turn our backs on it, to acknowledge defeat, but to hold on with determination. We find ourselves engaged in a tricky, driving game of wills. The more Poe eludes us, the more determined we become to know, to get to the center of the puzzle he presents. An encounter with Poe is fraught with paradoxes, however, one of which explains in part why the critical reader is reluctant to speak of that encounter: the more one attempts to answer the questions posed, the more one is forced to reveal oneself. In terms of the present discussion, one must reveal to what extreme lengths one will go when offered a puzzle. Some years ago, after reading an earlier version of this chapter, a friend commented, "You remind me of a dog worrying an epistemological bone." There is a cutting truth in that remark that is bound to injure a critic's dignity. One does feel like an arch Paul Pry and is haunted by the sense that there is something unholy about the quest, even something perverse. Yet there seems to be no way around the situation if we are to confront Poe directly. Having chosen to give up the comfortable security of cousinship, of comfortable distance, we must stand in a closer relationship to Poe.

It is not the theme or the subject of the text that is under scrutiny but the reader's relationship to the text. Engaging the text in this way, we become Poe's brother and are forced to play the alternating roles of victim and victimizer that he assumes in all his fictions. As soon as we assent to an involvement with Poe's language, we become victims of it. Every question we raise affords just enough satisfaciton to encourage us to try another. Asking more and more all-embracing questions, our metaphors grow increasingly abstract. Not long after the game begins, we come to feel embarrassingly like the interrogator in "The Raven," who finds himself, if not wildly, at least insistently propounding queries. Poe described the calculated effect he sought in this poem in "The Philosophy of Composition":

> And here it was that I saw at once the opportunity afforded for the effect on which I had been depending—that is to say, the effect of the *variation of application*. I saw that I could make the first query propounded by the lover—the first query to which the Raven should reply "Nevermore"—that I could make this first query a commonplace one—the second less so—the third still less, and so on—until at length the lover, startled from his original *nonchalance* by the melancholy character of the word itself—by its frequent repetition—and by a consideration of the ominous reputation of the fowl that uttered it—is at length excited to superstition, and wildly propounds queries of a far different character—queries whose solution he has passionately at heart—propounds them half in superstition and half in that species of despair which delights in self-torture—propounds them not altogether because he believes in the prophetic or demoniac character of the bird (which, reason assures him, is merely repeating a lesson learned by rote) but because he experiences a phrenzied pleasure in so modeling his questions as to receive from the *expected* "Nevermore" the most delicious because the most intolerable of sorrow. Perceiving the opportunity thus afforded me—or, more strictly, thus forced upon me in the progress of the construction—I first established in mind the climax, or concluding query—that query to which "Nevermore" should be in the last place an answer—that in reply to which this word "Nevermore" should involve the utmost conceivable amount of sorrow and despair.[7]

This is a half-comic rendition of the hermeneutical experience of Poe's reader. The questioning process does take this form. One begins by asking questions of a critically orthodox nature, examining themes, exploring symbolic patterns; one soon discovers that such questions yield results only up to a certain point. Then, as Poe says, the only further answer received from the text is "Nevermore." In the critical experience, however, it is the spatial element, "never *more*," that receives the emphasis. Every construct applied to the work can only be carried so far, and then it comes up against the covert statement of limitation that is stated explicitly in "The Raven": "Only this and nothing more." The reader is given enough material in the text to impose a structure, but the structure always remains open-ended. The "something more" needed to finish it, to round it off satisfactorily is never provided.

If we continue to query, however, it is not because we derive a perverse pleasure from being thwarted. Rather than expecting to be blocked repeatedly in our interpretive efforts, we go on hoping to model a question that will overcome or sidestep the difficulty. The solution appears to lie in casting our questions in a larger framework, and, as a result, we ask increasingly abstract questions. Correspondingly, they assume a more serious nature. Like the lover in the poem, we begin innocently and disinterestedly. But as our questions begin to raise serious epistemological issues, it is difficult to maintain an objective stance.

We soon realize that the text has invited and anticipated the critical response outlined above. If we are willing to play the game long enough, our reward is a flashing glimpse of a world both awesome and dismaying in its unity. It is awesome to see that not only each of Poe's stories but the whole body of his work forms an endlessly expanding yet, paradoxically, totally self-enclosed world, a world fluctuating between hope and despair, power and powerlessness, vision and the failure of vision. Our dismay resides in the apparent impossibility of capturing the nature of this vision. It rests in the process and therefore is never at rest. Moreover, it leaves us at our moment of most intense involvement with that vision at a level of abstraction that seems utterly divorced from the actual text.

The techniques that Poe employed to create his aesthetic resemble those later used by certain avant-garde writers in the cubist period. All of them follow the same pattern of a rapid alteration of the mind between a greatly expanded and narrowly contracted state of attention.[8] Roger Shattuck says in *The Banquet Years* that this technique was used by Satie in composing music and by Jarry and Apollinaire in literature to force the listener into a state dominated by the "logic" of the subconscious. Jarry, he claims, "pushed systematic absurdity into the realm of hallucination, of violated consciousness."[9] Reading Shattuck's chapter on Jarry, one is reminded continually of Poe, and Apollinaire's summary of the effect of Jarry's prose can as well be applied to the effect that Poe's prose creates as it transcends the objective reality of the text:

> There is no term to apply to this particular elation *allégresse* in which lyricism becomes satirical in which satire, directed towards reality, so overreaches its object that it destroys it and rises to a level that poetry can scarcely attain. Meanwhile triviality turns out to be in perfect taste and even, by an inconceivable state of things, becomes necessary. The Renaissance alone allowed such orgies of intelligence in which sentiment plays no part, and by a miracle Jarry was the last of those sublime debauchees. (*Il y a.*)[10]

Before turning to our text, *The Narrative of Arthur Gordon Pym,* let us look briefly at one further problem that arises in dealing with Poe. As a writer, Poe has been condemned for producing an art that is cold and calculating; on the other hand, he has been condemned for a compulsiveness and obsession that severely limited his work by leaving him only barely in control. In the first case, the artist is cast in the role of victimizer; in the second, in that of a hapless victim. Both states occur in his fictions, and there is some danger in attributing either one or both of them to Poe himself. Recent criticism tends to consider Poe a highly self-conscious, calculating author. The emphasis has moved away from the image of Poe as a powerless creator of landscapes that buried him alive to an image of Poe as the landscape artist who quite clearly recognized the nature he had to work with and consciously exploited it.

If the latter, more modern stance produces errors in judgment, it can hardly be more shortsighted than the earlier view has proved to be. We might argue that we are only taking our cue from Poe's Dupin. In an illuminating discussion of Poe's detective stories, Daniel Hoffman has shown that Dupin succeeds where the Prefect of police fails because Dupin never underestimates his adversary. Dupin, he says, sidesteps "the self-imprisoning assumptions" of the Prefect that lead him to view the Minister as a fool and thus infer that he can only act in certain ways.[11] Any reader closely acquainted with Poe can find a good many reasons for raging at Poe, but none would be inclined to berate him as a fool. Nevertheless, this was D. H. Lawrence's position in his otherwise fine essay on "Ligeia." This is a story, we are told, of spiritual vampirism, of two mutually destructive protagonists probing mercilessly into one another's soul. The two vampires in the story are Poe and Ligeia. Poe, the masculine side of this unsavory team, "set up his will against the whole of the limitations of nature. This is a brave man, acting on his own belief, and his own experience. But it is also an arrogant man, and a fool."[12] Poe certainly set up situations that pit the will against the limitations of nature. That he was brave and drew upon his own belief and experience, I concede. I will even concede that he was arrogant. But Poe was no fool. He was certainly not foolish enough to try to show nature's limits by making a real person (himself) the lover of a created character (Ligeia).

It is the critics—and Lawrence is the best instance—who have insisted that Poe is the hero of his fictions. In one sense, Poe *is* the hero of his fictions and closely involved in them, but he is also their creator. If he had to bring Ligeia back in the story, it was not because he was driven to continue to vamp her but because he knew, just as Lawrence did, that there is no end in this kind of struggle for knowledge. Poe and Ligeia, Lawrence claimed, "couldn't laugh. They were frenziedly earnest."[13] It is true that Ligeia never laughs; what captivates her humorless lover, however, is the unfathomable expression of her eyes. Could it be that the expression is one of humorous mockery? Poe can laugh, and among the most disturbing things about reading him is that one is never sure when he is laughing and when he is not. It is only Lawrence, not Poe and Ligeia, who is frenziedly earnest here.

If I laugh at Lawrence for falling into the Poe trap of being driven into a state of frenzied earnestness, I do it with certain reservations. As a student of Poe, I have found myself drawn into that state of mind too often to laugh with impunity. Besides, there will be plenty of opportunity to laugh at myself, at Pym, at Poe, and at man's pretensions to any kind of final and comprehensive knowledge as we journey through the pages of what Poe called "a silly book," *The Narrative of Arthur Gordon Pym*.

* * *

Angered by a letter in *Fraser's* attacking Poe's character after his death, William Gowan wrote a tribute to Poe, defending his conduct and character. His opinion, he said, was based on the best evidence, that of an eyewitness, for he was a living companion of Poe during his and Virginia's residence in Mrs. Clemm's New York boardinghouse. Gowan attested to Poe's sober habits and hard work: "During this time he wrote his longest prose romance, entitled *The Narrative of Arthur Gordon Pym*. This was the most unsuccessful of all his writings, although published by the influential house of Harper and Brothers, who have the means of distributing a single edition of any book in one week, still it did not sell."[14]

In fact, much of *Pym* was written in Richmond before Poe came to New York. Two installments had appeared in the *Messenger* (January and February 1837), carrying the story to the point at which the mutineers aboard the *Grampus* overpower the crew. But it is true that the book was unsuccessful. Almost to the present, it has suffered from a bad press and has been held up as documentary evidence that Poe was incapable of writing a sustained piece of fiction. It *is* a study in failure: not Poe's, however, but man's. And though Baudelaire calls the source of man's failure original sin, Poe had his own special term for it, perversity.[15]

The notion of perversity and the term *perverse* appear as early as 1831 in Poe's writings. It does not emerge as a full-fledged doctrine until some years later in "The Black Cat" (1843) and "The Imp of the Perverse" (1845). In the former, it is defined as the spirit that causes man to act against his own best interests in full knowledge of what he is doing: "the perpetual inclination, in the teeth of our best judgment, to violate that which is *Law*, merely because we understand it to be such . . . this unfathomable longing of the soul to *vex* itself—to offer violence to its own nature—to do wrong for the wrong's sake only."[16] In "The Imp of the Perverse," it is made even more explicit and appears as the urge to undermine our relationships with others by the use of convoluted language, as the impulse that causes us to delay action until it is too late, and finally as the drive to annihilation that overwhelms us if we dare take thought when standing on the edge of a precipice.[17] It permeates language, action, and thought. It is not any specific act, only the inclination to act against our own good. The protagonist-narrator of "Loss of Breath" can see suicide as his "good" and reject it on the grounds that "it is a trait in the perversity of human nature to reject the obvious and ready, for the far distant and equivocal."[18]

The reader of Poe is always in danger of acting perversely on two fronts. He must surrender himself to the fiction and alternately achieve a degree of detachment from it. G. R. Thompson describes this stance as one of "ambivalent self-division."[19] Just because *Pym* is one of Poe's few extended works, it allows us to see clearly the movement of perversity, for our state of ambivalent self-division is never a static one. We range from complete immersion in the text to an objectivity that is nearly devoid of emotion. At every moment we actively participate in undermining our position in order to swing back to its polar opposite. The movement back and forth between these two poles occurs over and over again and sweeps us into the pulsations of hope and despair. This movement can be rendered metaphorically by the simple physical act of the pendulum swing of a clock or by the rhythm of breathing, with inspiration as the rising hope and expiration as a sinking into despair or a kind of death. It can be rendered as a psychological principle, a will to self-destruction. It is theological when interpreted as the impulse to sin. Aesthetically, it produces a principle that results in stories destroying the forms that give them life. Because the movement is so pervasive, it is little wonder that Poe chose to spell it out in terms of the cosmos itself, that he saw perversity as a principle governing the movement of the entire universe.

In *Eureka* Poe described creation as a continuous movement between the two poles of the One and the particular. It is a process of differentiation, but that differentiation is strictly limited. Atoms emerge from the One to form a particular thing. However, their "appetite" for participating in the lesser unity of distinct forms can endure "only up to a certain epoch."[20] As their drive for differentiation subsides, a counterforce takes over, destroying the lesser unities of particular things, driving all matter back to the original Oneness that it possessed. As matter subsides, it does not return to a central globe of gigantic proportion. Rather, final Unity, matter without attraction or repulsion, contracts into a nothingness, "into that Material Nihility from which alone we can conceive it to have been evoked, to have been *created* by the Volition of God."[21]

According to Poe, the collapse of the material world into nothingness is not a matter for despair but for hope. The law of periodicity suggests that this process is one of renewal rather than one of final and total annihilation:

> Guiding our imaginations by that omniprevalent law of laws, the law of periodicity, are we not, indeed, more than justified in entertaining a belief—let us say rather, in indulging a hope—that the processes we have here ventured to contemplate will be renewed forever, and forever, and forever; a novel Universe swelling into existence and then subsiding at every throb of the Heart Divine?[22]

Many readers, emerging from the "novel" universe of *Pym* and the short stories, feel little of Poe's optimism. On the contrary, they feel that a world of endless process, a process ultimately divorced from meaning, is a matter for despair.

Eureka is not merely a case of a writer dabbling on the side, eccentrically modifying nebular theory. Nor is it a completely serious attempt to explain the universe. What it renders, and accurately so, is the created linguistic world of Poe's fiction. According to Quinn, "What he says of the divine creation is hardly more than an analogous description of artistic creation and that of a kind which he himself tried to practice."[23]

What Poe set forth here is a kind of cosmic aesthetic. Repeatedly enacted in the short stories, and in *Pym,* it operates in the following way. In every story we find ourselves at first in an intimate relationship with the narrative voice. Even when we know or suspect from the first that the narrator is mad, we are pulled into this relationship by other appeals. In "The Tell-Tale Heart," for example, after admitting that he is dreadfully nervous, the narrator entices us into his fiction by inviting us to "observe how healthily—how calmly I can tell you the whole story."[24] Always we find we have been deceived. As we move through the story, we disassociate ourselves from the implied intimacy of the narrative voice because that voice begins to betray itself. The betrayal takes a form of extravagance or excess. Either the cool, calm narrator reveals that his mind is distorted or the mad though controlled narrator repulses us with a horrible deed. Even in the more realistic fictions, we often encounter a realism carried to such an extreme that we reject the narrator for his lack of imagination. This is precisely the movement described in *Eureka.* As the narrative voice reveals the distortions of its mind, it becomes more and more differentiated. And as the revelation grows, so does the counterforce of revulsion in the reader's mind, causing him to pull back and check the unity or intimacy he shared with the narrative voice.

The Poe short story is carefully drawn to create a unity of effect. Time limits the differentiation of matter in the universe, and time—the length of the story—governs the unity of effect. Once the effect has been elicited, the short story, like differentiated matter, collapses. This literary collapse is conveyed figuratively by an act of confession, of self-exposure (see, for example, "The Tell-Tale Heart" or "The Black Cat"), or by a form of physical annihilation (the collapse of the house in "The House of Usher," the sea's swallowing up of the narrator in "MS. Found in a Bottle"). *Pym* is especially useful for a study of Poe's aesthetic because of its length. As an extended piece of prose, it reveals the periodic element described in *Eureka* by presenting us with a long series of collapses and recoveries, deceptions and revolts.

To begin, then, let us examine two instances in which the reader is drawn into this movement. Early in the book Pym introduces us to his dog, Tiger, and says, "Most people love their dogs, but for Tiger I had an affection far more ardent than common."[25] The reader therefore expects to hear a great deal more about the dog in the course of the story, and he does hear something more of him during the episode when Pym is trapped in the hold of the *Grampus.* Yet shortly afterward, Tiger disappears from the text, and no explanation or comment is ever made by his ardently affectionate master. This could be due to careless writing; it could also be part of Poe's continual thwarting of the reader's aroused expectations. On a broader level, the same process is at work in the final presentation of the large, white figure rising out of the mist. As James Cox notes, the play on the symbol of whiteness has led the reader to a state of "absurd speculation"[26] and, we might add, expectation, which collapses with the abrupt ending of the book. Yet once the reader has learned to recognize this movement of deception and rebels against it, refusing to fall blindly into the traps laid for him, a new dimension appears in the work. The book can then be seen as both carefully contrived and very humorous. One is no longer forced to write *Pym* off merely as Poe's abortive attempt at a structured novel. On the contrary, one must ask if Poe really intended *Pym* to be other than it is, an illustration of the process of creation and destruction of literary form.

Poe provided us with a metaphor for the apparent lack of symmetry in *Pym* when describing a portion of the island Tsalal. Like the land, the fiction is "strewn with huge tumuli, apparently the wreck of some gigantic structures of art; although in detail no semblance of art could be detected" (230–31). The two main episodes, those involving the *Grampus* and the *Jane Guy,* parody and ultimately wreck the illusion created by romantic and realistic modes of expression. In the *Grampus* episode, we are finally driven to revolt, to reject Pym for his excessive romantic wallowing in his own emotions; in the *Jane Guy,* Pym's devotion to realistic detail begins innocently enough. As we read on, however, it is revealed to be as destructive as the first mode, and Pym becomes for us a kind of stupid Dupin. The long neglect of *Pym* attests eloquently to the fact that "no semblance of art could be detected." It is this element of unapparent control, of hidden manipulation, that Poe admires in Defoe: "Not one person . . . in five hundred has, during the perusal of *Robinson Crusoe,* the most remote conception that any particle of genius, or even of common talent, has been employed in its creation! Men do not look upon it in the light of a literary performance. Defoe has none of their thought—Robinson all."[27] If this was the effect that Poe was seeking, he was, in a sense, unsuccessful. Pym has none of the critical reader's thought, Poe all. Until quite recently, the obtuseness and lack of control that is characteristic of the narrator, Pym, has been attributed to the author, Poe.

The reason for this mistaken identity is a failure to separate the two voices present in the story. The device of first-person narration deceptively draws us into an intimate relationship with the voice of Pym. As with all unreliable narrators, the burden of rejecting this intimacy is placed upon the reader. In order to achieve the distance necessary to distinguish the narrative voice from the implied authorial voice, the reader must experience the process of deception and revolt that characterizes the entire narrative.

Significantly, the first deception, the first enticement into fruitless speculation, concerns the discrimination of styles or voices. Pym, the ostensible author of the preface, tells us that Mr. Poe has written the first few pages and that "it will be unnecessary to point out where his portion ends and my own commences; the difference in point of style will be readily perceived" (3). Here the distinction we are invited to make is between two narrative voices. The irony of the appeal is that we must distinguish between the two voices—but not on this level and not on Pym's terms. For in fact there is no point early in the narrative where a shift in style occurs. We soon realize as well the absurdity of Pym's relying on belief from family and friends, "who have had reason, through life, to put faith in my veracity" (1). In the first portion of Pym's life that the reader is allowed to witness, he is anything but truthful. He and Augustus deceive the Barnard family in the incident with the *Ariel.* Pym deceives his grandfather when he encounters him in disguise on the way to the *Grampus,* and he must practice deception, including a fraudulent letter, against his entire family in order to make the voyage.

Yet as we recognize the absurdity of these two statements, we are in fact acknowledging Poe's projected authorial voice. Although at this point we could as well attribute the absurd irony in the two statements to Pym's voice as to Poe's, as we move through the novel we see that Pym *is* obtuse, that he is exposed as incapable of either irony or humor.[28]

In the first main episode, we reject Pym as we perceive his exaggerated sensibility. At first we are inclined to excuse him, to accept the justification for his actions that he offers in each case. When he confesses that the hypocrisy he practiced on his family disturbed him and was only "rendered tolerable to myself by the wild and burning expectation with which I looked forward to the fulfillment of my long-cherished visions of travel" (19), we are also inclined to exonerate him. Again, when he is so overcome by emotion that he cannot answer Augustus to save his life, we accept the situation. Nevertheless, an uneasiness accompanies our acceptance at this point because we see the whole thing as a bit ludicrous. If he couldn't speak, we ask ourselves, why didn't he bang on a box? Even if our sympathy for Pym survives this second crisis, it can hardly endure that of the cannibalism episode. Pym is appointed to hold the lots. He goes to one end of the ship to arrange them and is so overcome with cowardice that he prolongs the agony of anticipation for his three companions. Even after they beg him to get on with the task, he pauses to try to figure out how he can cheat one of the others into drawing the shortest splinter: "Even then I could not bring myself to arrange the splinters upon the spot, but thought over every species of finesse by which I could trick some one of my fellow-sufferers to draw the short straw" (128). Disgusted as the reader may be, he is immediately thrown on the defensive by Pym's justification: "Before anyone condemn me for this apparent heartlessness, let him be placed in a situation precisely similar to my own." However, if one backs off from the emotional intensity of the moment, the excuse Pym offers becomes highly comic. In the first place, this is not *apparent* but *real* heartlessness. In the second, there isn't one chance in a million (or more) that anyone would ever find himself in a situation "*precisely* similar" to Pym's. Pym is not asking that we judge leniently but that we not judge at all.

If the reader judges and maintains the distance needed for judgment, he can appreciate the satire aimed at Pym just a few lines later. Peters and Augustus having drawn two of the long straws, the lot must fall to either Pym or Parker. Without a trace of irony Pym tells us, "At this moment all the fierceness of the tiger possessed my bosom, and I felt toward my poor fellow-creature, Parker, the most intense, the most diabolical hatred" (128). Pym is not writing as the events transpire but as he looks back, and in hindsight he can say "poor" Parker. Even so, he is not aware of the ridiculous element in his metaphor: "tiger" conjures up the incident of the dog in the hold, and we see Pym metaphorically not as an enraged jungle beast but as a mad dog.

And there are other instances of Pym's unwitting use of irony and humor in his language. The most obvious example is his description of Dirk Peters, whom we are told is "one of the most ferocious-looking men I ever beheld" (51). He is short in stature, his limbs are rigid and bowed. His hands are thick and broad, hardly retaining a "*human* shape." His head is large and hairless, the mouth stretching from ear to ear and the teeth protruding. As the description runs on, the alert and distanced reader is forced to realize that Pym, unaware, is describing an ape, not a man. The inventive reader will realize that *A P E* is an anagram of *E A P,* the author's initials. Reading in this manner, we can see that the statements that follow are richly satirical, this time Poe aiming the satire at his own public reputation. "Of this singular being many anecdotes were prevalent among seafaring men of Nantucket. These anecdotes went to prove his prodigious strength when under excitement, and some of them had given rise to a doubt of his sanity" (52).

By the end of the story, Pym, like the *Grampus,* has been reduced to a stripped hulk filled with little more than shifting, sliding emotions. And yet this image of Pym slips away from us as quickly as the whole atmosphere of the *Grampus* and the emotion of the events that took place on her slip away from Pym. When Pym and Peters are taken on board the *Jane Guy,* there is no immediate relating of any word of the adventure to those on board. Instead, we are immediately inundated with facts about the *Jane Guy,* her captain, and her destination; we have been plunged into a new fictional illusion. We find ourselves listening with complete confidence to the voice that narrates the description of the ship. If we remember the shattered image of Pym with which we were left at the end of the *Grampus* episode, we remember it the way Pym and Peters remember their experience, as a frightful dream somehow lacking in reality. Referring to what happened on the *Grampus* after several pages of realistic description, Pym says,

> I have since found that this species of partial oblivion is usually brought about by sudden transition, whether from joy to sorrow or from sorrow to joy—the degree of forgetfulness being proportioned to the degree of difference in the exchange. . . . The incidents are remembered, but not the feelings which the incidents elicited at the time of their occurrence. (150)

At this point, the reader is hardly better off than Pym or the *Grampus* and equally in need of rescue. His long battle has not been with the sea and a mutinous crew but with a verbal environment that continuously shifts and slides beneath his feet. He has been buffeted by puns whose only purpose seems to be to scatter his energies and divert his attention from the text on which he is desperately trying to keep a grip. At the same time and at the other extreme, he must struggle against a mesmerizing alliteration that hammers at his sensibilities and dulls his responses. He has also been swung violently between skepticism and belief with nearly every twist and turn of the story. Each objection he raises to the implausibility of an event or feeling is allowed to fester in his mind momentarily—until the text counters it with a barely satisfactory but often painstaking explanation. Like the captain of the *Penguin* in the opening story of the *Ariel*, the captain of this literary vessel is careful "to make amends . . . for his atrocious behavior in the previous portion of the adventure" (13). The amends are always enough to keep the reader forging ahead toward the South Pole, oblivious to the now well-known feeling of despair that has taught him repeatedly that to arrive at a single pole is not to arrive at an answer.

The world of the *Jane Guy* at first appears to offer the reader a welcome respite from the stormy emotional world of the *Grampus*. The narrative voice is calm and sober. Yet the solid world of facts, longitudes and latitudes, flora and fauna, that this voice reveals is no more stable than that of the *Grampus*. The apparent care for factual detail and the reader's efforts to follow the directions indicated is mocked by the revelation that none of the islands sought is found and by Pym's remark in a note four chapters later: "I cannot, in the first portion of what is here written, pretend to strict accuracy in respect to dates, or latitudes and longitudes, having kept no regular journal until after the period of which this first portion treats. In many instances I have relied altogether on memory" (179). Again we find ourselves in the process of disassociating ourselves from the close proximity of the narrative voice. The major cracks in the illusion it creates occur at approximately the same places in the story of the *Jane Guy* as of the *Grampus*.[29] Here we discover a lack of imagination, not excessive emotional intensity. The first hint that this Pym lacks imaginative powers is given in the incident involving the discovery of a canoe fragment upon which "Captain Guy fancied that he made out the figure of a tortoise, but the resemblance did not strike me very forcibly" (177). Whereas the voice of the *Grampus* episode has too much wit in the Lockeian sense of the word, this voice has too little and gradually reveals itself as that of a stupid Dupin. Pym cannot comprehend the savages' reaction to four harmless objects—the sails, an egg, an open book, a pan of flour—and reveals that he lacks the capacity for the simplest inductive reasoning, despite having noted their negative response to the white skin of the crew members.

Again we find Pym writing his own apologetic. Having been responsible for urging Captain Guy to continue south to Tsalal, where all except Peters and he are killed, Pym says,

> While, therefore, I cannot but lament the most unfortunate and bloody events which immediately arose from my advice, I must still be allowed to feel some degree of gratification at having been instrumental, however remotely, in opening to the eye of science one of the most intensely exciting secrets which has ever engrossed its attention. (178)

We never learn of Pym's divulging that secret to anyone. Supposedly the text records it, but, of course, the text's ending is lost and with it the secret. Once again, Pym's justification is no justification at all.

Here too Pym lacks humor. In a passage that parallels the burlesque of Poe as ape, the savages perceive the ship in terms of a living creature, and the language used in the description suggests an upside-down human figure (182–83). There is a great deal of play on the word *arms,* the "big guns" are treated with awe and respect, and descending below, the leader of the savages, Too-Wit, is confronted by two mirrors that are most certainly eyes. Pym is in no position to perceive any of this and sees such a response as an "affectation." Nevertheless, the ironically distanced reader realizes that the outburst of laughter with which the savages greet the ship is the only possible response at this point. Similarly, Too-Wit's reaction to the "eyes" in the cabin below metaphorically recapitulates the reader's own experience. Seeing himself framed in one mirror, the savage turns to flee, only to find himself confronted by a second mirror. So, too, the reader freeing himself from the frame of Pym's voice, the description of the ship, finds himself within the frame of the author's burlesque of his own human figure.

A second metaphorical passage at the end of the chapter reinforces the notion of separate visions or voices. Referring to Too-Wit's experience with the mirrors, Pym compares it to the white men's reaction to the water of Tsalal. Upon first examination, the water appears murky, but a closer look reveals that it is "as limpid as any limestone water in existence, the difference being only in *appearance*" (186). He also notes that the water is made up of many separate and distinct purple-hued veins, which can only be separated if a knife blade is "passed down accurately between" any two of them. Then, "a perfect separation was effected, which the power of cohesion did not immediately rectify" (187). The description is a metaphor for the division of voices that must occur in the reader's mind so that he can perceive the limpid quality of this otherwise murky novel. It is also true that after each such separation there is a time lag of noncohesion during which he reads two voices. This doubleness disappears only as the fictional illusion of Pym's voice again gains control.

At this point, the cohesion is not reestablished so quickly that we miss the ensuing humor. The destruction of the illusion here closely parallels that in the *Grampus* story. First we begin to question Pym's judgment. Next we are presented with the burlesque figure of the writer upside-down or ape-like. The section is closed by the satirical comment upon this structuring, by the author's poking fun at his own method. For at the beginning of the next chapter, Pym expresses a deep uneasiness at the lack of accident in what is going on, saying his distrust arises from things appearing to have too much system.

After this second emergence of the projected authorial voice, Pym's voice fails to regain the kind of controlling attention it commanded at the beginning of the *Jane Guy* episode. The relationship between Pym and Peters mirrors this gradual but final separation of Pym's and the projected author's voices.

At the beginning of the book, the relationship between the two voices was very close, a closeness metaphorically represented by the Augustus-Arthur relationship. The two boys share the same school and the same bed. They become doppelgänger figures one for the other. Pym tells us, "It is probable, indeed, that our intimate communion had resulted in a partial interchange of character" (18). Augustus here represents the immersion of the authorial voice in the character of Pym. As Pym's double, he controls the course of events and initiates action. But when Pym emerges from below decks, a force in his own right, Augustus withdraws from him, slowly fades, and dies. Their relationship is gradually replaced by that of Pym and Peters. For a brief time, Pym-Parker acts and Peters only remains a shadowy sidekick. But small actions by Peters keep intruding, forcing us to begin acknowledging his good judgment. We see that his voice is to be trusted and not Pym's. The culmination of Peters's emergence for the reader occurs in the chasm scene. Peters's conjectures about the hieroglyphs (as artifact) undermine Pym's specious arguments for their being caused by natural accident. His coolness takes them down the cliff and saves Pym from his own perverseness. Peters metaphorically embodies the distant, controlled authorial voice. The emergence of the controlling force represented by Peters coincides with the reader's growing awareness of the controlled, ironic voice in the work.

The stories of the *Grampus* and the *Jane Guy* are bordered, respectively, by the story of the *Ariel* and the unfinished episode of the canoe heading into whiteness. Each of these two shorter sections capsulizes one of the two voices. The *Ariel* episode provides a metaphorical rendition of the involved, experiential voice. The emphasis on intoxication, the sinking into oblivion, renders precisely the reader's reaction to the seductive pull of the fictional reality created by Pym's voice. Hoax or not, the fictional illusion in *Pym* is very powerful. In spite of all the cracks in its surface, we find ourselves succumbing with sensations much like those of Augustus: "In one of our conversations Augustus frankly confessed to me, that in his whole life he had at no time experienced so excruciating *a sense of dismay* as when on board our little boat he first discovered *the extent of his intoxication,* and felt himself sinking beneath its influence" (16, italics mine).

In the canoe journey at the end of the book, we find Peters in a state diametrically opposed to that described by Augustus. Emotional involvement hardly exists. Peters responds to the "region of novelty and wonder" with apathy. He at least avoids the trap of being pulled into the illusion again or being seduced into an "absurd level of speculation." His position is that of the second, disassociated voice, the position of the reader reading at the ironic level. Pym tells us, "And now, indeed, it would seem reasonable that we should experience some alarm at the turn events were taking—but we felt none. The countenance of Peters indicated nothing of this nature, although it wore at times an expression I could not fathom" (240). We may conjecture that the unfathomable expression on Peters's face is one of humor or amusement, an emotion that throughout the book Pym finds difficult to understand. And it is integral to Pym's involvement that he lack the distancing, structuring element presupposed by the stance of humor.

We find ourselves finally in a position outside of Pym's world. Our recognition of the humor in the story has allowed us to disentangle ourselves from the text. Here we might conclude that *Pym* is a story written purely for entertainment, and, having extracted it, we are free to go on our way. But there are several things that work against such a response. Laughter accounts for only one of the polar experiences found in the text. It represents the hope we repeatedly experience but consigns to oblivion the equally real and present sense of despair that permeates the work. The only justification for choosing to emphasize the humorous side of the text is that it corresponds to Poe's position in *Eureka,* in which he tells us that the process is a reason for hope of eternal renewal rather than despair. Yet this choice seems to be purely arbitrary. It can only be made at the cost of ignoring what T. S. Eliot describes as the tremendous tensions generated in Poe's work and modern works that follow it—ignoring the element that creates "an increasing strain against which the human mind and nerves will rebel."[30]

A second reason for our reluctance to conclude that *Pym* is written purely for the sake of humor is the nature or kind of laughter that is evoked here. It is not of the sort that one rests in or finds cathartic. From the simple level of senseless pun to the final enticing of the reader to figure out for himself the Hebraic-based hieroglyphs in the chasms, the laughter evoked is accompanied by a grimace and a sense that one has been dealt with unfairly. Humor is often used to reveal human limitation, but in the House of Poe the cards are stacked and every game is crooked. One is invited to speculate with the seeming promise that evidence will be forthcoming—"the difference in point of style will be readily perceived." Yet no evidence follows. This can be seen not only as a matter for laughter but also as reason for resentment, for what is conclusively proved about man's limitations in such an absurd world?

If we choose, we can take *Pym* as a practical joke of which we are the victims. To do so, we must block out the rhetorical aggression so integral to the text and close our imaginations to the image of Fortunato, another victim. Otherwise, we see ourselves, like Fortunato, in cap and bells, walled in by Poe's language and crying "Ha! ha! ha!—he! he! he!—a very good joke indeed—an excellent jest. We will have many a rich laugh about it at the palazzo—he! he! he!—over our wine—he! he! he!"[31] We can take this position, but we are fully aware that it represents a willful blindness to the serious side of the text. Some readers, their response dominated by the resentments aroused by Poe's methods, refuse to see the humor. Resisting any further temptation to speculate, they turn their backs on Poe's world and flee from its declared absurdity. The narrator of "The House of Usher" believes that such a retreat is the most expedient solution. It would seem that all the critical gestures that can be made have been anticipated by other characters in Poe's fictional world. The recognition of humor in the text takes us outside Pym's angle of vision but not outside Poe's. The question is, then, can we find a critical position outside Poe's world? Or has every critical gesture that can be made been anticipated and therefore confined within the fabric of Poe's universe?

We have these difficulties with Poe's texts because built into each is the self-imprisoning assumption that the creative act and, subsequently, the creative response are entirely willful. We do not approach the text with this assumption, but, like the lover in "The Raven," our first nonchalant question and its answer result in our quickly becoming enmeshed in and ruled by it. E. H. Davidson attributes the horror and fear in Poe's world to the struggle of the will to survive.[32] I have shifted the emphasis, however, attempting to show that this struggle is present not only in the work but that it extends to and determines the rhetorical relationship between the authorial voice and the critical reader.

Davidson finds that two irreducible themes dominate Poe's writings. Sidney Moss summarizes these two themes as "a solipsistic self that would make 'reality what the inner will ordains' " and as "a questioning self that would pierce the pasteboard mask of appearances and thereby apprehend ultimate reality."[33] The themes correspond to the two voices or critical gestures that I have described in *Pym:* the self intoxicated by the illusion and the distanced, ironic self that frees itself from Pym but not from Poe. The result is a hermeneutical nightmare. The work provides us with an abstract framework on which we are invited to hang our particular, personal versions or visions of a world dominated by the struggle of the will to assert itself. Consequently, as Moss rightly argues, much of the thematic criticism applied to Poe's texts takes on the quality of a Rohrschach test: "We may learn a great deal about the critic's psyche in this way, but what we learn about the literary work is another question."[34]

This is the reason that thematic criticism conveys an impression of insularity, verging on solipsism. We can all agree that Poe created a nightmare world, but little agreement has been reached about the content of the nightmare. Lawrence claimed that the nightmare is about incest. Hoffman sees it as a return to the womb combined with the thwarting of the desire to return. Others have identified it as a study of obsession. Examples of this kind can be multiplied, yet each claims to be the irreducible theme that accounts for and encompasses all the others. To escape from this dilemma, we turn to more abstract descriptions of the content. Deception-revolt, passivity-power, attraction-revulsion, innocence-experience, Nu-Nu–Too-Wit: each set of terms is an analogical variation on Poe's central but elusive thematic movement. Again we are faced with the problem of choosing among them. In effect, we have only translated the problem from concrete terms to more abstract ones.

The reader may object that there is no justification for treating these themes reductively. In fact, Poe's aesthetic continually urges us in this direction; the apparently reductive nature of theme in Poe is integral to the hermeneutical nightmare he creates. American symbolist practice plays a nimble game with the idea of likeness in the metaphorical transaction. The relationship between any two things compared is repeatedly pushed to the verge of complete identity with only a fine hairline separating us from the final step. In the hands of Emerson, this tendency is used positively—to teach us the spiritual unity of all things. Poe exploits the technique to instruct us in the dangerous implications of egotism that are potentially inherent in such practices. For Poe has shown us that stepping over that fine line produces total unity in which both significance and particularity are sacrificed to oblivion. We awake in a world of will that is devoid of any objects upon which to exercise that will.[35]

Ultimately, our estimate of Poe must always contain some ambivalence. He is Emerson's dark angel, and his work is perverse. Yet perversity itself is a virtue in Poe's hands. If it undermines and destroys the self that strives to reach a larger and more beautiful reality, it also undermines and destroys the dangerously solipsistic self that is an equal partner, the soul's doppelgänger, in all such efforts at transcendence.

II. James: More than Melody

> After a long period of silent watching, the voice slowly and with characteristic deliberation said: "Bill, remember that no captain ever makes port with all the cargo with which he set sail." A long pause. "And Bill—remember—there is always another voyage."
>
> —Henry James to William James, Jr.[1]

I believe that *Pym* was largely shaped by Poe's love-hate relationship with the transcendental element of the American culture of his time. It would be foolish to argue, however, that James was driven by the same obsessive force in writing *The Sacred Fount*, a book in many ways echoing *Pym* in its themes and methods. For James had the advantage of a remove in both time and place from the aesthetic doctrines that were so prominent in the life and thought of the American Renaissance. This is not to say that James was not compelled to face their implications and to bring the problems they posed to some kind of resolution.

Transcendentalism offered an idea (correspondence) and a method (symbolism) for attributing significance to the external world. And although it claimed by its method only to bring to light significances that were already present, the role of the perceiver was crucial. The importance of that role is embodied in the premise that all men must become poets. But if transcendentalism followed the democratic system in its emphasis on the individual, it failed to incorporate an analogous system of checks and balances on individual perception. American writers quickly recognized the dilemmas it raised. Unchecked, perception might well carry the seer to a realm of transcendent vision. Unfortunately, as Poe realized, there were few restraints in a fallen world to prevent that vision from being displaced by the vision of an absurd, isolated world of nightmare.

The novels of the middle years, of which *The Sacred Fount* is the culmination, radiate an increasing sense of unease, of what might even be termed dis-ease. The social circles of Nanda, Maisie, and Fleda form a darker and more demonic background for the innocent protagonist than is found in the novels of the earlier period. The innocent protagonist, as J. A. Ward has pointed out, has fewer "good" persons to lend support. Moreover, due to its isolated opposition to the corruption that surrounds it, innocence or goodness often appears grotesque. Most unsettling of all is that innocence itself is called into question. Whether active or passive, it is portrayed as having an inherently destructive force.[2] *The Sacred Fount* illustrates these darker possibilities in their most extreme form. Initially, the reader finds himself in the presence of a seemingly innocent and naive narrator confronted by a sophisticated and corrupt society. The imbalance is soon righted. Before we are finished with the book—or we could say before the book is finished with us—the "innocence" of the narrator is seriously called into question; his innocent idealism partakes of the very characteristics of vampirism and adultery that mark the society around him. In fact, he evokes Poe's narrators, who, appearing rational at first, draw the reader into an intellectual intimacy only to reveal the insane twist of their minds.

We might see this movement toward ambiguity and the absurd as the crucial phase in James's development as an artist, as that period of struggle so often dramatized in the body of an author's work when he moves from a relative innocence to a more mature vision of his world. In James's case this larger archetypal pattern of development can be particularized as a confrontation with the problem of American symbolism, and Arnold P. Hinchcliffe points to *The Sacred Fount* as James's first significant excursion into a truly symbolic method.

> The novel is weak because it is the most difficult link in the evolution of the symbolic novel. *Madame Bovary* had ended the novel and in a sense begun the novel, and although James

> was initially under the spell of Flaubert and Turgenieff, he moved away from the realist novel and adopted a more American mode of writing akin to the romances of Hawthorne and Melville.[3]

Hinchcliffe believes that James failed in this experiment because the symbols used in *The Sacred Fount* are too derivative, the mask borrowed from Melville, the portrait from Hawthorne. I disagree with Hinchcliffe's reason for the failure but agree with his conclusion: "In the narrator with his not-so-simple tropes and figures and his detailed path to apparent craziness, there is perhaps a touch of premonition in a James about to tread the same path, saved only by the impersonalized regulation of a dynamic symbolism."[4] James was more conscious of the nature of his experiment than Hinchcliffe implies. There is no attempt at impersonalized regulation in *The Sacred Fount*. That was only to emerge from the experiment, to lend an aura of superb control marking the narrative point of view in *The Ambassadors,* which immediately followed, and in the intricate and finely wrought novels of the later phase. In *The Sacred Fount,* James allowed the demon with which he had to contend largely to have its own way.

If the critical language appears extravagant here, we might recall that R. P. Blackmur places the novel in the category of James's ghost stories, in which, he said, certain obsessions become the base for moral imagery and in which a kind of exorcism takes place.[5] Blackmur is rather vague about what is being exorcised in this novel, but it is fair to say that one of the objects of exorcism is the potential for intellectual anarchy that Feidelson saw lurking in an unlimited symbolism.[6] The mask-portrait symbol in *The Sacred Fount* illustrates the characteristic ambiguity found in other expanding symbols in American literature: Hester's *A* or the figure of Pearl in *The Scarlet Letter,* the whale in *Moby-Dick.* But the symbol is introduced and discussed in chapter 4 and then drops almost entirely from view. The problems raised by American symbolism are not exorcised by means of this symbol but by the book itself, which comes to stand for, to symbolize, the difficulties inherent in all symbols. It is a symbol of all symbols, which perhaps accounts for the fact that several critics have called

The Sacred Fount a metanovel. It is in this capacity that James used the novel both to explore the limits and to expose the limitations of American aesthetics. Or, to put it in a more positive way, James here (borrowing a line from Feidelson) "saves symbolism by symbolizing all that can be said for and against the symbolistic method."[7]

He began confidently enough—the thing was to be "the merest of *jeux d'esprit*," "a *consistent* joke."[8] Yet, begun as an anecdote, the book quickly overstepped its limits, expanding from fifteen thousand to eighty thousand words, the material exerting, James said, "a rank force of its own."[9] Nor was there any promise of an end to its unchecked vitality. Like many of the products of the transcendental aesthetic, it threatened to become an endless dialogue. For all his confidence in the role of the artist and his avidity for aesthetic experiment, James emerged from the whole experience chastened and slightly embittered. He was to refer to the finished product as "a profitless labyrinth," a book that "isn't worth explaining and I mortally loathe it."[10] One can only conjecture that he also emerged with a deeper understanding of Poe's voyage into the absurd as well as Hawthorne's and Melville's lapses into silence. Elsewhere he repudiated its method of first-person narration, condemning its "terrible fluidity of self-revelation."[11] Perhaps he repudiated *The Sacred Fount* as Poe years before had rejected *Pym* because it so much revealed the dark side of the aesthetic problems facing any author attempting to write in the "American mode."

At first glance, this novel might seem an odd candidate for the work in which James struggled with peculiarly American problems. The story is set in England and involves English characters in an English country house. But the shadowy, nameless narrator-recorder of the piece has often been consciously or unconsciously identified by critics as American. He has often been identified with James himself, and the work correspondingly has been viewed as self-satire or self-parody. We tend to identify him as American not because he resembles James—there are some resemblances—but because the epistemological dilemmas in which he entangles himself seem particularly American. His frenzy to know and his determination to know that he is right in his perceptions (even at the cost of seeming rude, boorish, and slightly crazy) strike the reader as very un-English.

We too are drawn into this quest to know. But the object of our investigation becomes as much how the narrator knows as what he knows. We soon become aware that he approaches a dramatic situation with a method that, if not strictly transcendental, involves attitudes that are. One of the clearest and most apt descriptions of the kinds of mental (and moral) dilemmas engulfing the narrator is found in the writings of Theodore Parker. In his autobiography, Parker described the dangers awaiting transcendental thinkers who rely too exclusively on their own intuitions, ignoring the checks and balances of other opinions and other facts. Speaking of his own experience, he wrote, "How often the inquirer mistakes his own subjective imagination for a fact of the universe. It is for others to decide whether I have sometimes mistaken a little grain of brilliant dust in my telescope for a fixed star in heaven."[12] In the essay "Transcendentalism" he described a second error that can arise when the transcendental method is applied without caution: "Men have scorned observations, have taken but a few facts from which to learn universal laws, and so failed of getting what is universal, even general."[13]

The two errors are present in the narrator's method of thought from the very start. He says that Gilbert Long is good-looking but stupid and that his manners are none of the best. But Long, rather than "cutting" the narrator as we are told he has done before, comes to meet him in an open and friendly way, seemingly unaware of any former rudeness on his part toward our speaker. The narrator then tells us he discovers that Long is not as good-looking but far better mannered than he had remembered. This description is not easy to accept as objective, for the reader immediately suspects that the revised opinion of Long partly arises from the cordial reception given the narrator. Next, the narrator formulates a "law" of human nature, the one that expresses his vampire theory. Parker's words are apropos, for from a few observed facts (Mrs. Briss looks younger, Briss older; Gilbert Long is cleverer), the narrator concludes that love relationships deplete one party and strengthen the other. He embarks on an avid quest for the female guest (May Server) who is being depleted on Long's behalf. His disinterestedness in the quest is highly suspect. Later, when he writes the story of his weekend, he confesses that he cannot forget May Server. And in the first pages of the book, his remark to Gilbert Long—" 'What a lucky thing then,' I laughed, 'that, with Brissenden so out of it and relegated to the time-table's obscure hereafter, it should be you and I who enjoy her!' "—betrays perhaps more than the narrator intends about his attraction to Mrs. Briss.[14] One recalls Coverdale's avowal of his love for the meek Priscilla and his similar self-deception about the strong, sensual Zenobia.

The narrator is in fact very much involved in the vampirism he observes and later records in his story. He preys upon the other guests and is in turn preyed upon. If Mrs. Brissenden has achieved a new youthfulness at the expense of her husband's losing his, she leaves the narrator as well with a sense of depletion. He tells us, "I didn't after all—it appeared part of my smash—know the weight of her husband's years, but I knew the weight of my own. They might have been a thousand, and nothing but the sense of them would in a moment, I saw, be left me" (218). We suspect by the end of the novel that he has fallen prey in another sense; he is the victim of his own method. He has tumbled into the trap that, Parker warns us, awaits the transcendental moralist:

> Danger, too, that he take a transient impulse, personal and fugitive, for a universal law; follow a passion for a principle, and come to naught; surrender his manhood, his free will to his unreflecting instinct, become subordinate thereto. Men that are transcendental-mad we have all seen in morals; to be transcendental-wise, sober, is another thing. The notion that every impulse is to be followed, every instinct totally obeyed will put man among the beasts, not angels.[15]

The imagery of the text bears out this beast-angel dichotomy. When the narrator is not a "providence," a good angel protecting the victims (May Server and "Poor" Briss), he is a dog—"I seem to snuff up," thereby "picking up the scent" (35).

The language also supports the idea that this novel is concerned with the dilemmas raised by transcendental aesthetics. It partakes of the same dichotomy as the angel-beast imagery. D. W. Jefferson describes it as producing a text in which "transcendental verbiage mingles with the open zest of the scandalmonger."[16] The narrator places a high value on "talk" and prides himself on his (179). When he is not enmeshed in incongruous metaphors, his language takes flight in exaggerated transcendental phraseology such as the following:

> The beauty perhaps was only for me—the beauty of having been right; it made at all events an element in which, while the long day softly dropped, I wandered and drifted and securely floated. This element bore me bravely up, and my private triumph struck me as all one with the charm of the moment and of the place. (96)

This time and this place encourage a high idealism, "a secret thirst for the infinite" (120), even if, as the narrator worries in the next example, they fail to appreciate fully and threaten to check a "transcendent intelligence" like his own:

> This especial hour, at Newmarch, had always a splendour that asked little of interpretation, that even carried itself with an amiable arrogance, as indifferent to what the imagination could do for it. I think the imagination in these halls of art and fortune, was almost inevitably accounted a poor matter; the whole place and its inhabitants abounded so in pleasantness and picture, in all the felicities, for every sense, taken for granted there by the very basis of life, that even the sense most finely poetic, aspiring to extract the moral, could scarce have helped feeling itself being treated to the snub that affects—when it does affect—the uninvited reporter in whose face a door is closed. I said to myself during dinner that there were scenes in which a transcendent intelligence had no application, and that, in short, any preposterous acuteness might easily suffer among them such a loss of dignity as overtakes the newspaperman kicked out. We existed, all of us together, to be handsome and happy, to be really what we looked—since we looked tremendously well; to be that neither more nor less, so not discrediting by musty secrets and aggressive doubts our high privilege of harmony and taste. (114)

I have quoted the passage in full, though I have seen it quoted in an abridged form elsewhere. When the passage is abridged, the references to the newspaperman are omitted, and to omit them is to ignore that wherever transcendental verbiage is found in the text, the incongruous, the absurd is never far behind. The drop in language to the simile of the newspaperman renders the passage comic; the reference discredits and disrupts the keeping of the language. It discredits the narrator, too, but it leaves us asking at what cost we would maintain harmony and taste, whether we are willing to omit, to ignore our own aggressive doubts about the narrator, the musty secrets of the society that here surrounds us and the language itself.

To entertain aggressive doubts is in this context to share the narrator's vampirism. To doubt seems to offer the reader a point of view detached from the narrator, yet paradoxically it draws the reader into a closer identification with him. The situation is, or ought to be, oddly familiar: it resembles the vampiric relationship of narrator and reader in *Pym*. The similarities between these two books illuminate each of them; the differences throw into clearer focus two alternative treatments of the basic problems raised by American symbolism.

There is no evidence that James had *Pym* in mind when he wrote *The Sacred Fount*, but one can be fairly certain that, at intervals, he was thinking of Poe. More than one critic has found it feasible to characterize the narrator as a "stupid Dupin." His position as "house detective," his conviction of his superior intuition, his ability to read the minds of the lesser beings who surround him, his inscrutable method that often leaves the other characters and his reader completely befuddled—all echo the "virtues" of Dupin. Whereas Dupin excites admiration, the hero of James's story excites annoyance and irritation. He seems a buffoon, a ludicrous caricature of Dupin.

An explicit reference to Poe's work occurs in the narrator's final interview with Ford Obert. He asks Ford if the ladies have all departed, for he hopes that Mrs. Brissenden has remained below to help him complete his investigation. Ford assures him that they have all departed, "soared aloft": " 'Save, it struck me, so far as they may have left some "black plume as a token"—' 'Not, I trust,' I [the narrator] returned, 'of any "lie" their soul hath spoken!' " (144). It is only a single reference, a seemingly chance remark, and yet like so many remarks in *Pym* and in *The Sacred Fount,* it opens and flowers with "a certain rank growth," to cite James's phrase about the novel itself. Traditionally, we have been taught that the more knowledge we have of a thing, the greater our mastery of it. Not so with the problematical novel. Here we are thrown into a situation in which the more we know, the more we contribute to an unlimited explication. The more we know of Poe's aesthetic and of *The Sacred Fount,* the more complicated becomes the explication of a single line or reference.

The reference here is to "The Raven" and is from the penultimate stanza:

> "Be that word our sign of parting, bird or fiend!" I shrieked, up
> starting—
> "Get thee back into the tempest and the Night's Plutonian shore!
> Leave no black plume as a token of that lie thy soul hath spoken!
> Leave my loneliness unbroken!—quit the bust above my door!
> Take thy beak from out my heart, and take thy form from off my
> door!"
> Quoth the raven, "Nevermore."

On the simplest level, the narrator's remark carries a significance for himself and the reader that must escape Obert; the narrator hopes in the forthcoming interview to catch Mrs. Briss in a lie. We are never sure what that lie is—whether he wants her to admit that she and Gilbert Long have become aware of their roles as vampires and are conspiring to conceal both the role and their consciousness of it, or whether he hopes she will reveal that she and Long are lovers. But the choice of "The Raven" has further implications. As a study in hermeneutical method, the poem portrays not a situation in which answers are found or discovered but one in which the answer is given from the start and questions are shaped (in a rising crescendo of horror) to suit that answer. This context of the poem throws a shadow of suspicion over the narrator, because his method, too, has been to begin with an answer and then to ask questions that will lead to it. The narrator says, late in the book in reference to his sounding of one of the characters, "The answers had really only been waiting for the questions" (119). And, as in the rest of *The Sacred Fount*, our attention is thrown back on the narrator's method, to the problem of his motives in asking questions.

Furthermore, if Poe's aesthetic is one of seduction, we can anticipate much of the outcome of the impending interview with Mrs. Briss. The narrator's quest for the key, the final building block for his "palace of thought," is not forthcoming. The answer from Mrs. Briss will be fixed at a certain level just as the Raven's is: the narrator will be given a certain amount of information and nothing more. Like the reader of Poe and the reader of *The Sacred Fount*, the narrator can only partially build a structure. The material needed to make it complete is at the crucial point withheld.

There are other echoes of Poe and his stories here. One of Poe's chief seducers is the narrator who draws the reader into close intimacy and gradually reveals his madness. When, in the final nocturnal interview, Mrs. Briss tells the narrator he is crazy, he asks, "You found it so natural then—and you so rather liked it—to make up your mind of a sudden that you had been steeped in the last intellectual intimacy with a maniac?" (199). And when his crystal palace of thought is smashed, he, like the narrator of "Usher," feels he must flee from the house and find a place where the air is healthier.

There is one other connection to Poe that though ostensibly tenuous may prove as significant as any of these others. It is contained in the allusion to Ludwig, King of Bavaria. Jean Blackall, in *Jamesian Ambiguity and "The Sacred Fount,"* devotes a chapter to the allusion, demonstrating how much Ludwig's story was before the public in the years before and during the writing of *The Sacred Fount*.[17] She uses the Ludwig figure as a parallel to James's narrator, arguing that this similarity is one more reason for us not to take the narrator as a model of the serious artist. I am not entirely convinced by her rendering of Ludwig as the type of the artist manqué. What seems more striking is that the person of Ludwig provides the same difficulties of assessment for his biographers as the figure of the narrator does for the reader. Sympathetic critics cheer his efforts to transcend everyday life by imbuing it with the fruits of sensitivity and imagination; detractors satirize him as an escapist, a man insane. The attitude toward him is almost always one of ambivalence, and ambivalence seems to rest on the same issue in both cases: Are the figures we are considering false artists, or are they only failed artists, and are the two one and the same or different?

The same ambivalent evaluation, the same questions have been asked of Poe and his work (especially in the discussions concerning his poetry). What is interesting is that the real Ludwig explained his difficult life as Baudelaire was to explain his: "I believe for reasons which I will give you, that there is a distinct parallel between Poe's nature and mine." He went on to describe himself as "abnormally sensitive and excessively moral." Speaking for himself, he might well be speaking for Poe:

> If my reading and observation have not been in the wrong direction, much of the phenomenon which is called insanity is really over-sensitiveness. It is often hinted and sometimes openly declared, that I am a madman. Perhaps I am; but I doubt it. Insanity may be self-hiding. An insane man may be the only person on earth who is not aware of his insanity. Of course I, for such reasons, may not be able to comprehend my own mental condition, except in an exaggerated and unnatural way. But I believe myself a rational being. That, though, may be proof of my insanity. Yet I doubt if any insane person could study and analyze himself as I have done and still do. I am simply out of tune with the majority of my race.[18]

Poe, Ludwig, our narrator: figures not altogether certain of where the boundaries lay between the real and unreal, sanity and insanity, romance and realism, life and art. They built houses, fantastic castles, crystal palaces that rested on the imagined boundary line. Ludwig's are the only ones not to go smash. But our purpose here is not to study Ludwig's castles or the analogous personalities of these figures, but to examine the kinds of structures that emerge from this basic uncertainty about boundaries and limitations.

* * *

The structure of *The Sacred Fount*, like that of *Pym*, is top-heavy. To apply Apollinaire's phrase, it is a kind of orgy of intelligence or, more precisely, of epistemology. An inordinate burden of speculation rests on a text that has struck readers from the beginning as trivial. The most famous description of the book's top-heaviness and its tenuous subject comes from Rebecca West; she called it a "small mean story" that "worries one like a rat nibbling at a wainscot" as it tells "how a week-end visitor spends more intellectual force than Kant can have used in *The Critique of Pure Reason*, in an unsuccessful attempt to discover whether there exists between certain of his fellow-guests a relationship not more interesting among these vacuous people than it is among sparrows."[19]

What is fascinating is the way this "small mean story," superficially trivial and apparently barren, can generate through an unlimited symbolism multiple meanings that represent multiple points of view. The meaning of Melville's whale, as we know, depends very much on who—Ishmael, Ahab, Starbuck—is doing the looking. *The Sacred Fount*, following the American tradition of edifying and educational literature, is a kind of how-to-do-it manual on the subject of point of view. The points of view it creates reflect both extremes of the displacement principle, the same extremes as those encountered in Poe's aesthetic. Here the narrator represents both poles of the knowing self found in *Pym*. Viewed negatively, his vision—the meaning he assigns to the data of experience—is solipsistic, the rendering of a private nightmare unshared by anyone else. Positively, he is the courageous knower who would pierce the "pasteboard mask of appearances" to reveal the truth. The problem he represents is mirrored in analyses of the text. The critical reader limits his point of view and emerges with a version of the text that excludes certain vital aspects, or he bravely attempts the larger view and is thrust into the realm of parable, generating an abstract metaphorical reading that leaves far behind the concrete world of the text itself. The same problem is touched on by Blackall when she discusses the result of readers ignoring the comic aspect of the book: "Critics have therefore had to move at varying degrees above the text or to deal only with those portions of it which sustain their respective views."[20]

Now these two critical positions—the one narrowly restricted, the other abstracted at various levels above the text—are the only "safe" points of view. Any other involves the reader in the narrator's murky game. For despite the implication that this is a search for the real, the true, the narrative structure is designed to mask all but what the narrator would have us see. When Mrs. Briss at the end of the book claims to have disengaged herself from him by means of some new knowledge, he asks: "Do you owe your discovery, however, wholly to my system? My system, where so much made for protection . . . wasn't intended to have the effect of exposure" (209). The harried reader can only comply with a grim smile to her response: "It appears to have been at all events intended to have the effect of driving me to the wall; and the consequence of *that* effect is nobody's fault but your own." Note that he does not ask her what she knows but how she knows it. If she knows according to his system, she has not succeeded at all in escaping his vampirelike grasp.

As with the Poe text, the reader is confronted with the problem of achieving some kind of distance, of getting outside the system. Here again one realizes that the various positions taken are repeatedly revealed as vulnerable. Again and again the discovery that these positions have been anticipated undermines them. At every turn the reader finds himself a victim, the shadowy figure of the narrator hovering near his elbow and murmuring, "I knew you'd think that." For example, the reader, if somewhat reluctantly, identifies his own need to escape the narrator with that of Mrs. Briss. By the end of the book, she seems to offer the best hope for a model of disengagement; as the narrator acknowledges, she, of all the persons in the book, is "an opponent worthy of me." Yet during one of her apparently most successful moves at disengagement, their final interview, the narrator says, "I see. Yet . . . you're not at present—though you wish to goodness, no doubt, you *were*—away from me" (198). She replies that she doesn't care if she is not physically free of him since she now is mentally—she is "away from your delusions." The narrator continues: " 'You wouldn't, in spite of your belief,'—I smiled at her—'like to be a little further off yet?' But before she could answer, because also, doubtless, the question had too much the sound of a taunt, I came up, as if for her real convenience, quite in another place." The taunt is directed at the reader as much as at Mrs. Briss, and it is by just such taunts and teasings that we as readers have been led through the entire text. No matter what distance we achieve, we always wish we were a little further off.

The place where the narrator comes up is once again within his own system. Mrs. Briss and the reader follow him with a sense of personal foolishness (like Thoreau following the laughing loon on Walden Pond). His next question asks her and us to help him understand what allowed us to reject the intimacy of his voice—whether it was all of a sudden or whether our loss of confidence only emerged gradually. The point is again not so much whether her and our disillusionment is gradual or whether it occurs in a sudden moment, but in our responding to the question at all. Once we respond, and Mrs. Briss does, we again consent to enter into his game and to be victimized by the tortuous logic of his system. Yet even if our consenting to examine when and how we lost confidence in the narrator is part of his game, it is a response worth making. Whatever the narrator intended to affect, his system does have the effect of exposure. Tracing our efforts as readers to step outside this system results in exposing both the humor and the horror that, carefully protected by his prose, lurks beneath the surface.

The preceding discussion assumes a view of the narrator as himself vampiric. Such a view, however, is not immediately obvious to the reader. Blackall begins her argument by claiming that a divided interest in the two subjects of vampirism and the narrator's point of view weakens the book and creates many of its difficulties. Only late in her discussion does she reverse her position and state that the two concerns are one and the same, that the narrator is a vampire. A few critics have argued that the narrator is purely a force for good, refusing to entertain even the slightest suspicion about his methods. This is a good example of the masking effect of the prose. On first reading, the question of his theory—whether the relationships between the four main characters are vampiric—dominates our attention. Only with some effort can we ignore that pursuit and turn the spotlight on the narrator himself. When we do, as James K. Folsom states, "only two things gradually become clear: first, the narrator becomes increasingly convinced that vampires are operative in the world of Newmarch; second, given the narrator's definition of vampires, we as readers become conscious that there is at least one vampire in the book, and that this vampire is none other than the narrator." For it is the narrator who "darts from person to person throughout the course of the story, sucking nourishment from each."[21]

How we become conscious of this aspect of his character is another matter. In only one instance is he explicitly portrayed as vampiric. In his final meeting with Obert, fearing that Obert is losing interest in the quest, the narrator grasps his arm: "I laid my hand on his arm and held him a moment with a grip that betrayed, I daresay, the effort to keep my thoughts together and lose not a thread." He describes Obert's reaction: "He continued to look at me; then he gave a laugh which was not the contradiction, but quite the attestation, of the effect produced on him by my grip. If I had wanted to hold him I held him. It only came to me even that I held him too much" (151). Still, the reference is only marginally explicit and might easily be overlooked. The rhetoric of the narrator, laden with the suggestion of significance, tends to equalize the language and blur our perception of lines like these, thereby protecting him from such ugly imputations as the one we are now making.

It was W. D. Howells who provided us with a clue to seeing this side of the narrator:

> I wish [James] would leave his people more, not less, to me when I read him. I have tried following their speeches without taking in his comment, delightfully pictorial as that always is, and it seems to me that I make rather more of their meaning that way. I reserve the pleasure and privilege of going back and reading his comment in the light of my conclusions. This is the method I have pursued with the people of *The Sacred Fount*, of which I do not hesitate to say that I have mastered the secret, though for the present I am not going to divulge it. Those who cannot wait may try the key which I have given.
>
> But do not, I should urge them, expect too much of it; I do not promise it will unlock everything. If you find yourself, at the end, with nothing in your hand but the postulate with which the supposed narrator fantastically started, namely,

> that people may involuntarily and unconsciously prey upon one another, and mentally and psychically enrich themselves at one another's expense, still you may console yourself, if you do not think this enough, with the fact that you have passed the time in the company of men and women freshly and truly seen, amusingly shown, and abidingly left with your imagination. For me, I am so little exacting, that this is enough.[22]

Despite the teasing quality of Howells's remarks, his clue is a good one. Reading only the dialogue in the book, we become aware of three things. First, we realize how much the adversarial element predominates in each of the interviews. These conversations, for the narrator, can be seen as ego battles in which his chief goal is to establish that he is more conscious of the implications of what is said than his partner. What I have called his quest, the problem of the relationships among Long, May Server, and the Brissendens, seems of secondary importance. At times it appears to be almost devoid of significance, a mere vehicle for the narrator to establish his own superior cleverness and critical ability.

Second, we realize that this ego requires a victim on whom it can feed. As the book progresses, the narrator fears more and more that he will lose his audience. We have already touched briefly on his need to "hold" Ford Obert and his effort to keep Mrs. Briss thinking along with him. In the course of the book, he holds audience with each of six characters. Briss and May Server form a passive audience. He regards them as so "out-of-it," so lacking in consciousness, that he treats them with a patronage bordering on contempt. He finishes sentences for them, thinks for them, and regards them as soft wax in his hands. Lady John and Gilbert Long are more likely candidates for the kind of audience he needs. Both are conscious enough to be aggressive doubters. Unfortunately, neither of them possesses the sympathy he requires. Both reveal their lack of patience with him and his methods and summarily dismiss him with varying degrees of rudeness. Lady John asserts that she is "kind enough for anything," but she sees him as having "an imagination of atrocity" and refuses to play his game (124). She advises him: "Well, all the same, give up, for a quiet life, the attempt to be a providence. You can't be a providence, and not be a bore. A real providence knows; whereas you . . . have to find out—and to find out even by asking 'the likes of' *me*" (126). A providence, a superior consciousness, knows everything concerning people's relationships. A providence knows also that it is superior without proving the point by engaging in vampirelike games. The narrator rejects Lady John's sage advice, saying, "I already saw her as necessarily stupid because I saw her as extravagantly vain" (127). How little he has taken that advice is revealed in his retrospective vision: "It comes back to me that the sense thus established of my superior vision may perfectly have gone a little to my head." Gilbert Long shows less kindness. He comically subverts the narrator's theory that he (Long) is no longer rude and impertinent by replying to questions about Briss with the rude question, "Have you got him on the brain?" (33).

Ford Obert and Mrs. Briss possess, however, both the necessary imaginative ability and the sympathy to qualify as a fit audience. Like the narrator, they too have private interests to protect from exposure that will render them adversarial. Obert can be appealed to because he is an artist and has a concomitant pride in his imaginative powers. Mrs. Briss, in the narrator's view, must protect herself from being exposed as a vampire, equally guilty with Gilbert Long of victimizing another person in order that she may flourish. She may also be trying to circumvent the discovery that she and Long are involved in an adulterous relationship.

One of the first hints of the adversarial nature of the narrator's relationships with his "proper" audience occurs in chapter 5. Mrs. Briss arrives on the scene excited and triumphant, glorying in the powers of perception that have revealed to her that May Server is the woman involved with Long. The narrator resents her confidence, finding her successively proud, fatuous, cruel, possessed of a "simplified egotism" (60). He dislikes her being triumphant when her knowledge is only partial, when she is still so unaware of how she victimizes Briss. Sensing his resentment, she, in turn, accuses him of objecting to the competition. She has drawn too close, become too much like him. In fact, the charges of cruelty, of fatuousness, and of egotism that he mentally formulates against her are those the reader has formulated against him. She says to him, "So I all the more resent your making me a scene on the extraordinary ground that I've observed as well as yourself. Perhaps what you don't like is that my observation may be turned on *you.* I confess it is" (63). The speech contains all the elements of an ego battle. Mrs. Briss, by proving herself his equal in perception, is now a threatening force capable of turning the spotlight on him and exposing him to a critical view. She dominates the conversation throughout the chapter. At its close, however, he gains what he calls a short-lived triumph when she is momentarily disconcerted by their discovery of May Server—talking not with Gilbert Long but with Mrs. Briss's husband. The detachment that she has gained by seeming to think beyond him and that gives her a position from which to criticize him is itself short-lived. He sums up her recapitulation: "She recognized her agreement with me, yet looked as if she had preserved a certain measure of freedom. Then she handsomely gave up even that" (71).

In the final chapters, Mrs. Briss is forced to do pitched battle for her freedom. Just before that, Ford Obert fights for detachment and is roundly defeated. Chapter 11 opens with the narrator and Ford discussing the question of their detachment. The issue is ostensibly whether Ford has given up his interest in the narrator's quest. The narrator attempts to convince Ford that he, Ford, is responsible for the whole thing and therefore cannot back out. Ford's hints, he claims, fed his own interest and resulted in an interest that he characterizes as "this failure of detachment." He says, then,

> "What you said to me as we were going up yesterday afternoon to dress—what you said to me then is responsible for it. And since it comes to that," I pursued, "I make out for myself now that you're not detached either—unless, that is, simply detached from *me.* I had indeed a suspicion of that as I passed through the room there." (148)

As the chapter progresses, the narrator recaptures Ford by reawakening his interest in the quest. More important, he makes it clear that Ford is not only not detached from him but is once more put into a subordinate position. Ford's only means of detachment is to claim that he does not care, and the narrator so quickly enmeshes him in a renewed battle of egos that his avowal is rendered comic. The argument quickly moves from what Obert knows to how he knows it. The narrator points out that Ford knows the same facts that he does; because Ford lacks awareness of how he knows, because he does not have all the elements, he remains a step lower down on the ladder of perception than the narrator himself. The narrator tells Ford, "That's the sort of thing we just now spoke of taking a day for. At any rate, such as they are, these elements, . . . I believe myself practically in possession of them. But what I don't quite see is how *you* can be." Ford replies, "Why in the world shouldn't your analogy have put me? . . . I'm not an idiot either" (153). The narrator leaves Obert, not when he has proved him an idiot but when he has convinced himself that Ford has missed some of the elements and has brought Ford to the reluctant confession, "You do . . . know more than I" (163). Part of Ford's "defeat" is a result of a half-deliberate attempt on the narrator's part to mislead him. Ford is left with the false impression that it is May Server who will tell all to the narrator in his late-night interview, not Mrs. Briss. Yet despite the questionable means employed, we can still find Obert's failure comic. The only thing he stands to lose in the battle is his pride. If he suffers exposure, it is only the exposure of how he has missed certain links that make his perception less complete than the narrator's.

With Mrs. Briss the case is quite different. Were the narrator to win in the ego battle of the last few chapters, not only would her intellectual shortcomings be exposed but her moral shortcomings as well. He appears to conceive of the battle in the same terms as his duel with Ford Obert. Chapter 12 opens with the narrator's search for a flaw in her confidence. Images of profit and loss, the cost to the ego of each combatant in pride or humiliation predominate. He offends her by suggesting that it is his humiliation that she really seeks: "Of course, if you've got new evidence I shall be delighted to hear it; and of course I can't help wondering whether the possession of it and the desire to overwhelm me with it aren't, together, the one thing you've been nursing until now" (173). But if Mrs. Briss has been nursing anything, it is the realization that to win in this situation at all, she must divorce herself from his system. Merely to overwhelm him with her superior knowledge is to continue to play his game, and, win or lose, as long as he keeps her within his system he is victorious. As he points out, it is not whether they agree or disagree that creates the excitement for him but that they are working together. The one thing he cannot allow is a loss of audience: " 'You haven't with the force of your revulsion, I hope, literally lost our thread.' But as, in spite of my thus waiting for her to pick it up she did nothing, I offered myself as fairly stooping to the carpet for it and putting it back in her hand" (178). It does not matter then who lowers himself before the other so long as the literal quest continues and the ego game that rests upon it is sustained. By the end of the chapter, the narrator recognizes that Mrs. Briss is aware of his traps and is determined not to succumb as easily as his former opponents: "I paused for a reply, but they were not to come so happily as from Obert" (181).

Obert was easily recaptured and brought back to the fold. Mrs. Briss is determined to avoid recapture. Her first gesture is similar to that offered the reader in the Poe text. She renounces all further speculation. Because, as the narrator points out, the more one thinks, the more deeply one is enmeshed, she declares, "I must have stopped thinking!" (187). He immediately destroys this detachment by asking her to tell him at what point she stopped thinking, and, he notes, "She had to think even to do that." He then pretends to let her out of his system by granting her the privilege of being inconsistent. However, he attaches himself to her all the more firmly by turning the question of how she has detached herself into part of his own quest. If he is deluded or mad, he declares, she must show him where he has gone wrong. Mrs. Briss recognizes what he has done and charges him with insincerity. If he were sincere, she says in effect, he would abandon not only the literal quest but the ego game that he is so desperately playing with her. As she says when he asks her what he can do to convince her of his honesty, "You can easily prove it. You can let me go" (195).

Mrs. Briss wins the argument and her freedom—at the cost of the reader's sympathy. Seeing her driven and harried by the narrator's system of thought that attributes significance to everything, we side with her. Yet we are not willing to go all the way with her to the other extreme and conclude in opposition to him that "there's nothing in anything" (197). Nor are we convinced that she has "won" in the end by opposing to his system "her own now finished system" (218).

Howells's method does not unlock everything. It does, however, as he promised, make us more aware of the way that the principle of vampirism spreads out and pervades every level of the book, operating on at least three different levels. The narrator sees vampirism among his fellow guests; we become aware that it also governs the relationships between the narrator and each of his partners in conversation; moreover, it pervades the relationship between the narrator and the reader. The problems of detachment experienced by all the characters are analogous to those of the reader. Like the narrator, we broaden our perceptions, psychically and mentally enriching ourselves at another's expense. (In our case that other on whom we feed is the narrator.) Like his victims, we fight for detachment, attempting to establish a self-identity different from his. Yet the more we think, the more we seem to become enmeshed in an indiscriminate identification with our protagonist. Even our position as readers offers us no immunity. We are pulled in close, forced to be active participants in the fiction. If, as Edel says, the reader is the real detective, then he is also the real victim of the method provided him by the narrator.[23]

We can arbitrarily refuse to think, concluding that the book has no significance except to serve as a cruel joke perpetrated against its readers. However, there has been a persistent reluctance on the part of most critics, past and present, to assign *The Sacred Fount* to the category of the hoax, which would indicate a hostility toward and contempt for the audience that seem altogether alien to James as a practicing artist. It may be that we assume that James's repeated concern for the freedom of his characters extends also to his audience. Whatever the cause for our confidence in James, the effect is that most readers agree with Howells's refusal to "believe he is going finally to play me the shabby trick of abandoning me in the dark."[24] At the same time, we must remember that if James never abandoned us in the dark, he had no scruples about leading us to the edge of the abyss and confronting us with that darkness: the fate doled out to his freest and best-loved characters, who emerge from their experience chastened but more aware of the rigors and cost of judgment.

A rigorous education is the fate also of readers of *The Sacred Fount*, and we cannot claim that we were not forewarned. At the close of the first chapter, the narrator says:

> The difficulty for me is simply that if I've seen the handsome grow ugly and ugly handsome, the fat grow thin and the thin fat, the short grow long and the long short; if I've even, likewise, seen the clever, as I've too fondly, at least, supposed them, grow stupid: so have I *not* seen—no, not once in all my days—the stupid grow clever. (23)

Mrs. Briss replies, "All I can say is then that you'll have, the next day or two, an interesting new experience." The narrator's statement summarizes our experience of the text, and Mrs. Briss's statement conveys an overtone of the comic and an undertone of the sinister, both of which are very much a part of that experience. We begin on a certain note of levity, the same note of levity that the narrator is later to charge Mrs. Briss as having taken, only to discover that the cleverness of which we are fondly proud has led us into a labyrinth in which we feel profoundly stupid. If this were all, the book would be a hoax, the dark, dismal, despairing work that Blackmur thought it. Fortunately, we are allowed to see the stupid grow clever. Anything we learn from *The Sacred Fount*, however, cannot be expressed as a finished system. That kind of closed consistency must be reserved for the narrator.

Critics have quite naturally approached the text asking what James meant by it or what the text signifies. Existing critical commentaries show that this leads to an explication of the multiple visions that the text contains. It invites us to pick up any one of the innumerable threads that run through the book and follow it to its end. The problem, however, is that at the end of the book we hold in our hands a long thread of connections that tells us nothing of the weave and texture of the book itself.

The text demands a higher degree of self-consciousness

than is assumed in such questions. It does not present a meaning; it is a study in the problems that confront us in the assignment of meaning. Those problems are confounded by being set in the given context of the narrator's world. As in the aesthetic world of Poe, method has grown self-conscious. The text is reflexive, constantly commenting on its own processes. It contains, in Raymond Immerwahr's phrase, "a direct treatment within the narrative of the conditions of the narrative."[25] It invites us to make the same gestures that the narrator makes. But we are also constantly urged toward discrimination. As readers, we are asked, like Dupin, to become aware (if not free) of the self-imprisoning assumptions that are contained in a method become self-conscious.

To pick up any single thread and follow it involves us in just such an assumption. Although in any other context such a gesture might lead to vision, here it leads to obsession, or, more accurately, vision here equals obsession. Just as *vampirism* is given a particular meaning in the text, so is *obsession.* This is not to say that the reader himself becomes so engrossed in his particular chain of analogies that he willfully ignores other elements in the text. Rather, the text itself is so constructed that to focus on any single chain of analogies results in a masking; the creation of a single center of attention tends to block out or displace all the other elements that might possibly lay claim to our attention. This is illustrated in the discussion of Howells's method of reading. On first reading, we are so held to the question of whether vampire relationships exist among the four characters under the narrator's observation that we are effectively blocked from seeing that the vampirism extends to the narrator's relationship to those characters and even to us as readers.

This kind of thinking, a linear approach, involves us in a rigidly sequential, tunnel-like vision. It is what immediately traps the narrator and sets him on a predetermined course. He sees certain effects, Mrs. Briss looking younger, Briss grown old. To these effects he assigns a cause; his vampire theory is the result, and he is off on the chase. *Tunnel-like* is an appropriate adjective because this mode of vision is often humorously portrayed as his "train" of thought (72, 120). He earnestly endeavors never to miss a link in the chain of his reflections

(139, 163). He "sees" Mrs. Briss at the beginning of their final interview, at the end of a series of lighted rooms, "through a vista of open doors" (165). This rigid sequence is also echoed in the narrator's treatment of time. A good many of the chapters begin with a description of the first thing the narrator has done or that has happened to him. The cumulative effect of such beginnings raises to a parodic level the opening sentence of chapter 8: "I'm afraid I can't quite say what, after that, I at first did, nor just how I immediately profited by our separation" (96). His method reminds us of vacation slide shows given by people whose only means of organizing their experience is sequential: "first we . . . then . . . after that." But this "order and march" of things has its sinister side. Presented as a way to vision, it also has the effect of blocking vision. Its imprisoning effects are noted by the narrator when, gazing out at the stars, he says, "We had ignored them in our crystal cage, among our tinkling lamps, no more free really to alight than if we had been dashing in a locked railway-train across a lovely land" (142).

Several critics have taken the narrator to task for this kind of thinking. Robert Andreach describes the narrator's approach as based on either-or alternatives. His compulsive ordering of existence, Andreach says, results from a failure to distinguish between conceptual analysis and existential experience.[26] Folsom makes much the same charge: "He cannot conceive of any principle of life which is not rooted in the tangible world of cause and effect, however absurd this tangible world seems to appear. The trouble with his theory is not, as he thinks, that it is too inclusive, but that it is not inclusive enough."[27] There is a great deal of either-or thinking in *The Sacred Fount*. If it were all the narrator's thinking, we might easily enough entertain a vision of the text that effectively separated our perceptions from his. He would then be, as in one sense he is, a person with a "system, which he applied without discernment" (17).

There is in the text, however, a second mode of thought present, the relational, that works against the linear vision. Linear, either-or, thinking, Folsom says, leads the narrator to assume that for one person to live another must die; the narrator transfers his assumption to the picture "where he sees the mask and man as existentially connected." The relationship of man to mask is one of dependency like the other vampiric relationships in the book. Folsom asks,

> But is this inevitably so? If the man and the mask were both real—which they are not—they would not necessarily have more than an accidental relationship. Both the man and the mask could then exist independently. On canvas the relationship between the two is even more accidental, though at the same time it appears more real. When one views a painting, one is inclined to assume that its various parts have some meaning in reference to each other. But this is not necessarily the case. In many paintings, as it is only too clear in modern non-realistic art, the various elements are related to each other only as they relate to the picture as a whole. The only definition which can be given of such a picture, is a relational one, in this instance, that a man is holding a mask.[28]

Other critics have noted the relational or cubist aspects of the book. But to become aware of them does not, as Folsom seems to imply, guarantee us a place outside of the narrator's framework. Describing the "civilized state" of mind enjoyed at Newmarch, the narrator says,

> The perfection of that, enjoyed as we enjoyed it, all made a margin, a series of concentric circles of rose-colour (shimmering away into the pleasant vague of everything else that didn't matter,) for the so salient little figure of Mrs. Server, still the controlling image for me, the real principle of composition, in this affluence of fine things. (121)

In the text we are continually pulled away from a linear argument and enmeshed in a series of concentric circles of analogy. The disconcerting thing is that the controlling image or principle of composition (here Mrs. Server) is never stable. We are invited to take up and then abandon one controlling image after another. The narrator describes this movement in chapter 7: "A whole cluster of such connections, effectually displacing the center of interest, now surrounded me, and I was—though always intellectually—drawn into their circle" (72). It would be a simple matter if the linear argument were displaced by a single cluster of connections. What happens instead is that each cluster in turn becomes the center of interest and is displaced by others that arise from beneath the surface of the prose. Their variety is evident in critical accounts of the book. Hinchcliffe sees the book as dominated by images of flowers opposed by images of violence. Blackall records six metaphorical motifs that form the clusters—on the serious side: paying, sacrifice, and the sacred fount; the collection; the drama; and the picture—on the comic: games and the hunt. Other critics have noted the submerged religious imagery, a cluster that questions who one's neighbor is and speaks of retaining a priceless pearl and the gaining of the kingdom. These images proliferate as the reader's awareness of the text expands. They form a picture that we are urged to interpret by not losing any of the image clusters, a picture quite different from the one created by the narrator's romantic rhapsody over May Server and her setting in chapter 8. That picture bespeaks a carefully focused vision based on the stasis of an older aesthetic. This one is relational and full of moving clusters pointing to the aesthetic experience of cubist art. At the same time we are asked to arrange the proliferating motifs in a pattern of significance, our point of view is changed to allow one after another of these motifs to appear as the key, as the central point of focus. If we attempt to discriminate and give one of these clusters significance over all the others, we are forced into a restricted viewpoint that excludes the motifs working against that particular cluster. If we refuse to discriminate, we find ourselves in a labyrinth of conflicting significances or meanings, all of which seem to have equal claims.

Like the Poe text, James's plays with the boundary between analogy and metaphorical identification. From the beginning scene, in which we are given the equation (Mrs. Briss is to Briss as Gilbert Long is to May Server) that forms the narrator's "torch of analogy" to our realization of how difficult it is to separate ourselves from this narrator, we are presented with a mode of vision capable of an endless expansion. Yet we are continually made aware of the cost of assuming this singular way of seeing since the expansion depends upon a multiplication of analogies that masks the differences between things. Analogies in this context verge on metaphorical equivalence. When, following Howells's method, we discover vampirism on three levels—among the guests, between the narrator and each of the other characters, and in the relationship between narrator and reader—we are invited to assume a metaphorical identity, to see any one level of vampirism as equivalent to the others. As a result, asking any question of the text places us in the same position of metaphysical snoop as the narrator and forces us to assume all the other undesirable characteristics he possesses as well.

Howells touched briefly on the problem of the reader's entrapment, asking why we resent a work (like this) that has no central plan or final structure. Life, Howells said, often confesses itself to be without plan, and he wondered what right we have to demand more order of an imitator than we get from the Creator. He concluded, "Of course, it can be answered that we are *in* creation like characters in fiction, while we are outside of the imitation and spectators instead of characters; but that does not wholly cover the point."[29] It does not, to say the least, cover the point in *The Sacred Fount*. Our very problem as readers of this fiction is here defined, for the character with whom we closely identify is the perfect spectator. The method of the book makes it difficult for us to establish in what way we are not like the narrator, in what ways we are outside this fiction.

The same problem is writ small in the scene that portrays the characters attempting to interpret the picture of the man and the mask. I do not propose to offer yet another interpretation of that ambiguous portrait but to look briefly at how the course of the interpretation runs. The narrator offers the following description of the portrait:

> The figure represented is a young man in black—a quaint, tight black dress, fashioned in years long past; with a pale, lean, livid face and a stare, from eyes without eyebrows, like that of some whitened old-world clown. In his hands he holds an object, some ambiguous work of art, but that on second view becomes a representation of a human face, modelled and coloured, in wax, in enameled metal, in some substance not human. The object thus appears a complete mask, such as might have been fantastically fitted and worn. (50)

May Server and the narrator name the mask in the picture, respectively, the Mask of Death and the Mask of Life. What I would point out is that the man's dress and both faces—the man and the mask—are highly stylized and artificial. The painting is a representation of a face already a mask, about to assume or just having abandoned a second mask. It is thus remarkable that the four characters—May, the narrator, Long, and Obert—extend their interpretation by identifying these artificial faces, second view or not, with real persons. Similarly, confronted with the "extremely studied" picture presented by the book as a whole, we are urged to identify this picture with the various positions that the very real person of the reader occupies.

We are left with the question of how imitation works, of how art is *like* life. Whatever that likeness is, life cannot be totally identified with the representation that constitutes *The Sacred Fount*. The problems we face in dealing with the claims of the aesthetic are like those we face in dealing with the narrator. Both appear to glide easily over the distinction between representation and reality and to present us with the inclusive vision of an all-knowing providence. The same kind of objection that arises in us at this claim to inclusiveness was raised by Parker against Emerson: "He is sometimes extravagant in the claims made for his own method, and maintains that ecstasy is the natural and exclusive mode of arriving at new truths while it is only one mode."[30] (For Parker, ecstasy is the state of intuition in which man loses his individual self-consciousness.) As we have seen, our objection takes the form of attempting to retain our individual self-consciousness and to show how the narrator's vision is particular, a single mode of vision rather than an all-encompassing one. For we are only too aware, to borrow again from Parker's evaluation of Emerson, that this "man, who is the measure of all things, is not the complete man."[31]

Where then has James left us? As Howells predicted, we are not abandoned in the dark; rather, he has presented us with a definitive fiction that symbolizes all that can be said both for and against the American symbolist method. If his narrator's system is not designed for exposure, James's system is. And herein lies the difference between James's treatment of the problem and Poe's. Given the principle of perversity, one would expect Poe's aesthetic to betray itself, to expose the problems that arise when method becomes self-conscious. And in some ways it does. It is possible to see Poe as representative of the dark side of Emerson. It is even possible to think that Poe saw his work as betraying the difficulties of Emerson's aesthetics. After studying *Pym,* the reader should find it difficult to read the doppelgänger murder scene in "William Wilson" and not see it on one level as Poe's statement of the relationship between Emerson's art and his own. It concludes: "In me didst thou exist—and, in my death, see by this image, which is thine own, how utterly thou hast murdered thyself."[32] Nevertheless, though one may feel convinced that Poe saw his role as artist as a kind of martyrdom, as a writing against the predominant aesthetic of his age, there is no way to make a clear case for it. For in Poe's work, any gesture of rebellion—of perversity—is included within the framework of his universe. *Pym* raises a much greater anxiety in the reader because Poe had no scruples about trapping his readers in a dark world. By making every gesture of judgment a part of his aesthetic, Poe suggested that there is no alternative, that the aesthetic transaction that occurs is the whole of the discussion about art and life.

Critical discussions of *The Sacred Fount* reveal that many readers have chosen to see it in the same light, to move from the analogies it presents to an all-embracing analogy that makes it a statement about the artist's role or a parable of the relationship between art and life. Yet if we see it as a discussion of the problems raised by an unchecked analogous mode of vision, it is foolish to derive its final meaning from a further application of analogy to the novel. The text gives us enough information to feel uneasy about such an application, an uneasiness reflected in the argument that arises about how representative of the artist the narrator really is.

James made it less difficult for us to step outside his system. *The Sacred Fount* is the novel in which the reader comes closest to being a Jamesian character, and James extended to the reader the same aesthetic and moral attitudes and considerations that he extended to his other characters. Like Poe, he was willing to drive us to the wall and reveal the limits of our freedom; unlike Poe, he always refused to violate the final dramatic freedom of either characters or reader-characters. The work allows us to see that the narrator's method is only a particular method, one that by its very nature must make claims to inclusiveness. We can put a stop to the endless analogizing by concluding with Mrs. Briss that there is no meaning at all in *The Sacred Fount*. Or we can see it as a work that depicts one mode of transcendence while betraying the difficulties that arise from that method's necessary claims to being the only mode of art. There are a number of characteristics that emerge under these conditions.

A preoccupation with method is accompanied by a thin subject matter. Both texts, Poe's and James's, are top-heavy, the thought generated greatly outweighing the subject matter from which it arises. The device used to create this situation often takes the form of an ego battle in which the reader is urged to keep pace with the superior perceptions presented by the narrative voice and at the same time to disassociate himself from that voice. Sensing this identity struggle, some critics have tried to vindicate the narrator by characterizing him as a hero embarked on a quest for identity. Given this discussion of the work as an exploration of the problem of analogy as identification, it should be clear that *The Sacred Fount* is indeed about an identity struggle, but not one that allows us to champion the narrator or to blink an eye at his questionable tactics.

The text leads us to an expanded vision brought about by a continual displacement of the point of view, an endless shifting of the center of interest. Concomitantly, we are confronted with an invitation to judgment and a constant thwarting of that judgment. It is never allowed to rest secure, or, perhaps, it is never allowed to operate in a way that results in the elements of the text hanging together. We are repeatedly invited to organize all the facts into a "romantic," closed system, but that system is never allowed to be brought to completion. If we do complete it, we can be fairly sure that a little further thought will reveal an element unaccounted for.

The two kinds of dichotomy presented above are accompanied by a corresponding sacrifice of feeling. To keep our balance at all in this textual situation, we must struggle for distance and against any emotion that would pull us in close to the text. We are brought to the same realization as the narrator, that feeling is one of the things that must be let go:

> There were things that for so private and splendid a revel—that of the exclusive king with his Wagner opera—I could only let go, and the special torment of my case was that the condition of light, of the satisfaction of curiosity and of the attestation of triumph, was in this direct way the sacrifice of feeling. There was no point at which my assurance could, by the scientific method, judge itself complete enough not to regard feeling as an interference and, in consequence, as a possible check. (203)

We *are* allowed to feel the humor of the book; that humor, however, like the humor of *Pym,* is directed against us. It evokes a grimace as we repeatedly witness the exposure of our own limitations or watch the disintegration of our various crystal palaces of thought.

These elements all unite to form an aesthetic expression in which form predominates, in which method itself becomes the matter of the text. The assumption of transcendental aesthetics that form and matter are one and the same is here carried to its extreme limits, the formal convolutions of the text being its subject matter. The result is the creation, to recall Apollinaire's phrase once again, of works that become "orgies of intelligence in which sentiment plays no part." Such works seem to arise at those points in history when an expansion of perception has outstripped common standards of judgment.

We find ourselves reluctant to bring judgment against such works. Most of us would agree that a work that raises the consciousness of its perceivers is legitimately poetic. But our ambivalence about an emphasis on method expresses itself when we confront an aesthetic like Poe's or the aesthetic that informs *The Sacred Fount* and are forced to resort to less than laudatory terms like *technically perfect* and *a master of technique.* For what is gained, the cost seems too great. Ignoring Emerson's injunction to return to the natural fact plunges such works into analogical orgies. Perception for the sake of perception is James's narrator's justification for abandoning feeling. Certainly Emerson would have questioned the validity of this aesthetic, would have asked along with the narrator why those persons who enjoy a bright and insolent lack of awareness ought to "be made to begin to vibrate, to crack and split from within" (131).

James intended for us as well to return to the natural facts that constitute his story. Unlike the divers the narrator evokes in chapter 8, our diving ought to end with a reemergence on the surface. The facts to which we return at the story's surface might be termed unnatural facts, however, for in spite of all the efforts to mask them, vampiric and adulterous relationships exist at Newmarch. Along with its elitism, charm, and high cultivation, Newmarch ("new frontier") also possesses a high tolerance for the new style, the style of Mrs. Froome and Lord Lutley "and their servants too, like a single household—starting, travelling, arriving together" (19). These adulterous relationships are present in a text in which the relationship of form and matter is illegitimate, lacking the balanced harmony of true marriage. The narrator's concern for method creates a textual situation in which form depletes the material by taking to itself the qualities of matter. Something is gained for art in the transaction; the emphasis on form produces a narrative that contains entirely new qualities. The narrator describes this effect in terms of the relationship between Gilbert Long and May Server:

> It put before me the question of whether, in these strange relations that I believed I had thus got my glimpse of, the action of the person "sacrificed" mightn't be quite out of proportion to the resources of that person. It was as if these elements might really multiply in the transfer made of them; as if the borrower practically found himself—or herself—in possession of a greater sum than the known property of the creditor. (49)

But something is lost here, too. There is a loss of feeling, of the human and the personal. On the new frontier, the listeners have learned to appreciate "music without voice," which Poe, with his emphasis on music, would have applauded. James felt differently and concluded that a self-conscious preoccupation with form did not constitute the true marriage he sought to effect in his own art. After finishing *The Sacred Fount,* his words might have been those of Gertrude Stein, some twenty years later: "Melody should always be a by-product it should never be an end in itself it should not be a thing by which you live if you really and truly are one who is to do anything and so as I say I very exactly began again."[33] James "really and truly" was to do a great deal more. *The Sacred Fount* is the culmination of the middle phase. In the later phase, James must have drawn on the lessons he learned there. He returned to a more limited, controlled point of view, no doubt realizing, as he emphasized again and again in *The Fount,* that one always does so at a cost.[34] He did not choose to hang together in the sense of creating closed, completely accountable romantic fictions, but that had never been his way. Of one thing we can be certain; he never again chose to hang quite so loosely as in *The Sacred Fount.* On 9 August 1900, he wrote to Howells: "I have just finished as it happens a fine flight . . . *into* the high fantastic, which has rather depleted me, or at any rate affected me as discharging my obligation in that quarter."[35]

III. Hawthorne: The Fine Edge

> As for Septimius, let him alone a moment or two, and then they would see him, with his head bent down, brooding, brooding, his eyes fixed on some chip, some stone, some common plant, any commonest thing, as if it were the clew and index to some mystery; and when, by chance startled out of these meditations, he lifted his eyes, there would be a kind of perplexity, a dissatisfied, foiled look in them, as if of his speculations he found no end.
>
> —Nathaniel Hawthorne, *Septimius Felton*

The introduction to "P.'s Correspondence" ends with the narrator's comment upon P.'s desire for literary fame:

> P. had always a hankering after literary reputation, and has made more than one unsuccessful effort to achieve it. It would not be a little odd, if, after missing his object while seeking it by the light of reason, he should prove to have stumbled upon it in his misty excursions beyond the limits of sanity.[1]

The narrator, though sympathetic to P.'s dilemma, cannot endorse his "unfortunate friend's" methods for winning an audience and, subsequently, a reputation for himself as an author. Neither could the author of the story, Nathaniel Hawthorne, embrace such a solution to the problems of the American writer. For if we can accept any of Hawthorne's dicta as trustworthy, it must be the one that urges us to "keep the imagination sane."

Certainly Hawthorne was aware of the temptation to the absurd, the possibility of the exploitation of the demonic in American aesthetics. Moreover, he well understood Poe's experiments in that realm and felt himself deeply indebted to Poe as a literary predecessor. In his most complete statement of aesthetic practice, the serio-comic sketch "The Custom-

House," there is a strong evocation of Poe. The narrator emerges from the Custom House in a semimaddened state to "seize the public by the button" and inform that public of his three-years' incarceration.[2] Brooding above him during those years was "an enormous specimen of the American eagle" displaying "the customary infirmity of temper that characterizes this unhappy fowl."[3] In an admirable imitation of many of Poe's heroes, he finds himself in a state of torpor that "accompanied me home, and weighed upon me in the chamber which I most absurdly termed my study."[4] Part of the ostensible purpose of the sketch is to account for the narrator's coming into possession of certain documents that form the authentic germ of *The Scarlet Letter.* For these he is indebted to a Mr. Surveyor Pue, a man, he claims, "who might regard himself as my official ancestor." In a comic dialogue, the ghost of Mr. Surveyor Pue asks that he be given some recognition: " 'But, I charge you, in this matter of old Mistress Prynne, give to your predecessor's memory the credit which will be rightfully due!' And I said to the ghost of Mr. Surveyor Pue, 'I will.' "[5] But it seems wisest at this point to leave the Custom House behind and not to place an undue tax upon the reader's credulity.

Early critics seem to have been naturally reluctant to associate Hawthorne with Poe, a reluctance arising from the perception that these authors placed very different values on art and its relationship to the total scheme of man's moral endeavor. It was on just such grounds that James Russell Lowell condemned "a shallow criticism" that "has sometimes fancied a resemblance between [Hawthorne] and Poe."[6] The difference, Lowell went on to say, is that between a consummate "talent" and "genius," "between a masterly adaptation of the world of sense and appearance to the purposes of Art, and a so thorough conception of the world of moral realities that Art becomes the interpreter of something profounder than herself." My purpose is not to argue the merit or lack of merit in such an evaluation but to point out some of the effects it has on our assessment of Hawthorne's art. For many years American fiction possessed a dark angel, Poe, and set over against him a white angel, Hawthorne (the "blue-eyed Nathaniel" who so stuck in D. H. Lawrence's throat that the stuttering, staccato style of his two essays on Hawthorne resembles nothing so much as a bad fit of choking). There was concern lest the two meet, as if Hawthorne, like a snow-white Hilda, had to be protected from the dark imaginings of his sophisticated contemporary.

This contrast exaggerates, but there did exist a persistent tendency to box Hawthorne off, to attribute to him a fixity and simplicity, a naïveté, that his work proves he did not possess. Theodore Parker doubted whether Hawthorne "understood his own genius or comprehended the philosophical meaning of many of the circumstances or characters found in his books."[7] And E. P. Whipple wrote, "His great books *appear* not so much created by him as through him. They have the character of revelations,—he, the instrument, being often troubled with the burden they impose upon his mind."[8] The question they failed to ask was whether that appearance of revelation was a consciously cultivated effect sought by the artist.

The same attitude lay behind other attempts to limit the scope of Hawthorne's art and to keep him at a certain remove. It has been claimed that part of his simplicity resides in his emphasis on morality and his consequent use of allegory. Yet the moral dilemmas that confront us in his fiction are never simple, and anyone who has tried to impose a strict allegory on a Hawthorne story knows how quickly that device can come to be a cumbersome burden rather than an aid to any real understanding.

At other times, doubt of Hawthorne's intellectual depth took the form of lamenting his inability to deal with the present and the actual. Hawthorne, we are told, owing to his limitations, was able to write well only when his story was grounded in the past and kept within the narrow precincts of his native New England. By this showing, *The Scarlet Letter* is his most perfect work. Nevertheless, the later works, especially *The Marble Faun* and *Our Old Home,* which invoke the international theme, direct their sharpest denunciations at mid-nineteenth-century American society and its Pelagian bias. In the years just prior to the Civil War, Hawthorne, like an Old Testament prophet, pilloried a society that in its overweening confidence in its own innocence refused to see the destructive disunity it was about to bring down upon a political body ideally and orginally conceived as a perfect unity. Whatever the time or place employed in his stories, his chief concern was with the moral dilemmas that arise in a Christian democratic society.

To convey his message, Hawthorne developed an aesthetic that gave to his fiction a dim, vague quality. As a result of identifying too closely the writer with his fictions, critics took this misty atmosphere as an index to the quality of Hawthorne's mind. Hawthorne himself was aware of the tendency to evoke his personality from the distinctive character of his fiction. The character assigned to him on the strength of the stories and sketches later collected as *Twice-Told Tales* is that of a man rather effeminate and ineffectual. In the concluding paragraph of the preface to that volume, Hawthorne, with typical humor, enacts his assigned character in the very process of delineating it:

> This kindly feeling (in some cases, at least) extended to the Author, who, on the internal evidence of his sketches, came to be regarded as a mild, shy, gentle, melancholic, exceedingly sensitive, and not very forcible man, hiding his blushes under an assumed name, the quaintness of which was supposed, somehow or other, to symbolize his personal and literary traits. He is by no means certain that some of his subsequent productions have not been influenced and modified by a natural desire to fill up so amiable an outline, and to act in consonance with the character assigned to him; nor, even now, could he forfeit it without a few tears of tender sensibility.[9]

In light of the rest of the preface, Hawthorne appears to have been saying, "Better this assigned character than to have no character, no existence at all for the reading public." As might be expected, Herman Melville found it difficult to view Hawthorne's plight with either humor or equanimity. In his review of "Mosses from an Old Manse," Melville stressed the blackness in the fiction in an attempt to confute the public's image of a "harmless" Hawthorne.

> You may be witched by his sunlight—transported by the bright gildings in the skies he builds over you; but there is the blackness of the darkness beyond; and even his bright gildings but fringe and play upon the edges of thunder-clouds. In

> one word, the world is mistaken in this Nathaniel Hawthorne. He himself must often have smiled at its absurd misconception of him.[10]

More recent criticism has done much to correct the misconception that Melville lamented. There is now little or no resistance to associating Poe and Hawthorne. While Hawthorne is still viewed as a reluctant symbolist, nonetheless he is seen as joint inheritor with Emerson, Poe, Melville, and Whitman of the basic problems of romanticism and as one with them in the search for solutions.[11] It is this viewpoint that allows Charles Feidelson to conclude, "What seems at first a wholly personal problem, resulting from Hawthorne's peculiar temperament, turns out to be a reflection of the problem of the times."[12] Most important of all in this reassessment of Hawthorne has been the critical recognition of the emphasis on form in his work. Richard Harter Fogle's *Hawthorne's Fiction: The Light and the Dark,* Hyatt H. Waggoner's *Hawthorne: A Critical Study,* and Roy Male's *Hawthorne's Tragic Vision* all have as a central focus the formal organizing structures of Hawthorne's fiction. John Caldwell Stubbs, in *The Pursuit of Form: A Study of Hawthorne and the Romance,* locates himself within but extends this critical tradition by showing how the theory of the romance provided Hawthorne with guidelines for carefully structured works that, in turn, gave him a basis for further experimentation. More vigorously than his predecessors, Stubbs argues for Hawthorne's intentional use of and experimentation with formal structures, saying that Hawthorne "exerts much more control over his material than most critics are willing to admit and . . . his quite self-conscious shaping and the resulting lucidity are not detriments but rather the sources of his strength."[13] Two recent books, Edgar A. Dryden's *Nathaniel Hawthorne: The Poetics of Enchantment* and Kenneth Dauber's *Rediscovering Hawthorne,* also assume a self-conscious shaping, making formal patterns the keys to the central meaning of Hawthorne's work. Dryden attempts to avoid the limitations that emerge in thematic studies by defining a single encompassing movement, an unvarying pattern that occurs in all of the writings, in an alternating movement between enchantment and disenchantment. All the other themes are merely visions of this one, lesser variations of an approach to and withdrawal from the world. The subject or central theme then becomes the writer himself, "a self that may be defined simply as the organizing principle or conceptual center of this work."[14] Dryden's study is illuminating, but finally it suffers from the movement toward abstraction of which all thematic studies partake. The vacillating movement he describes is like that in Poe's fiction, and the method Hawthorne devised to break out of such circularity is ignored. To state it another way, Dryden fails to maintain his hold on the individual texts and on the individual author. The encompassing theme he discovers belongs to Poe and James as well as to Hawthorne.

Kenneth Dauber's study of form represents a radical departure from the critical tradition traced above by rejecting the idea of a transcendent theme or set of themes in Hawthorne's work. The fiction is performative, he argues; thus, "The referential quality of literature in Hawthorne . . . is but a necessary condition of literature as a tool of action."[15] Although I am sympathetic to Dauber's approach and agree with him on many points, the conclusions we reach are quite different. For example, in keeping with his thesis that Hawthorne's work lacks unity, Dauber argues that the vacant places created in the work by the juxtaposition of opposites are, indeed, vacant but that Hawthorne pretended such spaces are full. While I do not claim they are full, they point to a lost reality and by evocation bring it into a measure of being. Similarly, Dauber perceives in Hawthorne, as I do, a theory of art analogous to a theology of incarnation. For him, however, the experiment fails totally: "The 'Transformations' of *The Marble Faun* are, as it were, the word made flesh. No wonder, the reader asks, and quite legitimately despite Hawthorne's objections, whether Donatello has furry ears. The meaningless word inevitably cannot be understood, and the flesh is offered as its substitute."[16] Again, our differences might be seen as a matter of degree. I believe, and I think that Hawthorne himself came to believe, that his final experiment in form was largely a failure. However, to refuse to explore its partial success is to lose the flickering radiances that mark the boldest of his ventures in form.

Success or failure, Hawthorne continues to intrigue us. If

we have a somewhat greater respect than his earlier critics for the intricate rhetorical relationship he created between himself and the reader, still our desire to "place" Hawthorne (despite our frequent disclaimers) is reminiscent of theirs. Even as late as 1963, James Folsom could deplore the persistent and unwarranted identification of Hawthorne with one or another of his characters, a tendency most marked in *The Marble Faun:*

> Where ethical readings of Hawthorne's fiction generally go wrong is by proceeding on the assumption that in any given tale or novel some character is Hawthorne's mouthpiece, or that some ethical choice made by a character is that particular one which Hawthorne recommends. Thus, most of the criticism of *The Marble Faun,* for example, boils down to a rather fruitless and heated argument over whose explanation of the meaning of Donatello's crime we are to accept. Is the Fall fortunate, as Miriam suggests? Or in Donatello's fall are we damned all, as the pious and orthodox Hilda would have it?[17]

Our modern sensibilities may move us to favor Miriam's stance in regard to the Fall; nevertheless, our rhetorical stance resembles Hilda's less than orthodox position. Any bits of blackness that splash out of Hawthorne's deep fictions stain only our external garments; we remain unspotted and untouched within, as little transformed by the experience as Hilda herself.

We protect ourselves, perhaps with good reason, from the terms of the relationship Hawthorne extends to us. Discussing Hawthorne's use of tragic elements and their effects upon both characters and audience, F. O. Matthiessen points out that catharsis comes for his characters not only in their recognition of the inevitability of external events but also in an inner moral recognition of their own evil.[18] The latter was developed to the full by Hawthorne, Matthiessen claims, warning that such an emphasis "may seem an unwarranted transfer of the tragic catharsis from the audience to the protagonist." Matthiessen here unwittingly touches on a major circumstance in Hawthorne's rhetorical relationship with his audience. Hawthorne did intend his audience to experience a catharsis similar to that of his protagonists, to move from innocence through a fall to a higher state of awareness. But he was also concerned to place safeguards around us as a protection in the dark journey he invites us to undertake. As a result, the pressure is always to push catharsis inward: into the fiction and away from ourselves, toward the characters and finally to Hawthorne himself. Especially in *The Marble Faun,* the last complete novel, which demands even more reader participation than any that preceded it, we have been only too ready to accept Hawthorne's perhaps overscrupulous protection.[19]

* * *

Widely popular in the first few decades after its publication, *The Marble Faun* later sank into obscurity. Despite a revival of interest in the book over the last twenty years, the consensus is that the novel is a failure. The reasons given for its failure are both numerous and varied. Critics have pointed out that the four principal characters with the exception of Miriam are wooden and thus unrealistic. The most extreme case, Hilda, verges on the allegorical. All are supposedly transformed by their experiences in Rome; yet only Donatello seems markedly changed by the end of the book, and we are allowed to view his change only from outside his character. Furthermore, the book is filled with a disconcerting array of subjects. The virtues and vices of Roman Catholicism, women's role in society, nudity in art, the Fall of man, the decay of Rome, the democratic qualities of needlework: no subject seems too large or too small to escape the book's compass. Amid this weltering confusion of subjects, it becomes difficult to say what the story *is* about. It appears to consist of an endless series of dichotomies, set forth, commented on extensively, and finally left unresolved. This inconclusiveness, the lack of resolution, has bothered readers most. We expect a romance to provide us with a tighter structure, to round things off at the end in a way that never occurs here.

Even Hawthorne's first readers objected that there were too many loose ends. The result is the odd Conclusion or Postscript added to the book's second edition in which the "author" deprecates the literal mindedness of his readers. Those who ask whether Donatello had furry ears have missed the point. But the "author" then completely capitulates to this kind of reader, confessing that he has a similar curiosity. He becomes (in a single sentence) the person of the naive reader and a created character talking over the problems left unsolved with "his friends, Hilda and the sculptor." How fully he capitulates is revealed at the end of the interview: " 'Only one question more,' said I, with intense earnestness. 'Did Donatello's ears resemble those of the Faun of Praxiteles?' "[20] Like all the other misdirected readers, the "author" is rewarded only with a mysterious smile and a pun. "On that *point*, at all events, there shall be not one word of explanation."

A more serious criticism concerns the lack of resolution on a larger scale. Romantic characters and events are placed in a realistic guidebook setting. At times, the transition to guidebook language is so unsettling that one has the impression of reading two separate books bound by some mistake into a single volume. Note in the following passage how flat that language appears when it follows lines richly evocative of Milton and the ego's self-imprisonment.

> At intervals they looked through the lattice-work of their thoughts at the varied prospects that lay before and beneath them. From the terrace where they now stood there is an abrupt descent toward the Piazza del Popolo; and looking down they beheld the tall palatial edifices, the church domes, and the ornamented gateway which grew and were consolidated out of the thought of Michael Angelo. They saw, too, the red granite obelisk, oldest of things, even in Rome, which rises in the center of the piazza, with a four-fold fountain at its base. . . . And now that very obelisk, with hardly a trace of decay upon it, is the first thing that the modern traveller sees after entering the Flaminian Gate! (106)

Or again, after an emotional scene between Miriam and her model in which she kneels to him in a public square and begs for mercy, we are confronted with these words:

> There are three streets that, beginning close beside each other, diverge from the Piazza del Popolo towards the heart of Rome: on the left, the Via del Babuino; on the right, the Via del Ripetta; and between these two, that world-famous avenue, the Corso. It appeared that Miriam and her strange com-

> panion were passing up the first-mentioned of these three, and were soon hidden from Hilda and the sculptor. (109)

The weary reader, like a weary traveler, wonders at the necessity of there being a second- or third-mentioned way.

Although he repeatedly referred to the book as a romance, Hawthorne was aware of the odd blend of romance and realism that he sought to effect. At the beginning of the story the narrator says, "Viewed through this medium, our narrative—into which are woven some airy and unsubstantial threads, mixed with others, twisted out of the commonest stuff of human existence—may seem not widely different from the texture of our lives" (6). This statement is repeated and elaborated in the opening paragraph of the final chapter. Hawthorne's choice of a metaphor for his work, the figured tapestry, is strikingly similar to the "figure in the carpet" that James was later to employ. And his defense of the loose ends of the story is cast in the same terms as Howells's defense of James's *Sacred Fount:*

> The gentle reader, we trust, would not thank us for one of those minute elucidations which are so tedious, and, after all, so unsatisfactory, in clearing up the romantic mysteries of a story. He is too wise to insist upon looking closely at the wrong side of the tapestry, after the right one has been sufficiently displayed to him, woven with the best of the artist's skill, and cunningly arranged with a view to the harmonious exhibition of its colors. If any brilliant, or beautiful, or even tolerable effects have been produced, this pattern of kindly readers will accept it at its worth, without tearing its web apart with the idle purpose of discovering how the threads have been knit together; for the sagacity by which he is distinguished will long ago have taught him that any narrative of human action and adventure—whether we call it history or romance—is certain to be a fragile handiwork, more easily rent than mended. The actual experience of even the most ordinary life is full of events that never explain themselves, either as regards their origin or their tendency. (455)

The question here, of course, is whether the right side of the tapestry has been sufficiently displayed. As we have seen, most estimates of the book conclude that it has not. Rather, it is intimated that in *The Marble Faun* Hawthorne fell prey to the intellectual anarchy inherent in a system based on an endlessly expanding symbolism. Darrel Abel concludes his discussion of *The Marble Faun* with an assessment of Hawthorne that moves in this direction. Hawthorne, though never aiming at a complete philosophical system, "had one trait of the philosopher, which might be called an expanding consciousness: he never touched the limits of his reality, and although he had no urge to think his way through infinity, he had an urge to feel his way through it."[21] He carried his investigation of the problem of evil "to the largest observable patterns of life, and finally pushed his speculations beyond even these limits."

Such a conclusion is hard to accept. Everything in Hawthorne's fiction argues against this kind of Faustian role for the artist. *The Marble Faun* does appear to expand limitlessly, but our judgment of the book rests on whether we choose to see that expansion as a loss of control or as a carefully controlled technique aimed at achieving a very different end from that of Faustian speculation for its own sake. *The Marble Faun* does push romance to its limits. As we have seen in James and Poe, however, the technique of breaking form by pushing it to its extremity is, paradoxically, a means of reinforcing and defining limitations. Certainly, Hawthorne was as much aware as Poe and James of the problem of an endlessly expanding symbolism. In *The Italian Notebooks* we read that a picture may be "a great symbol, proceeding out of a great mind; but if it means one thing, it seems to mean a thousand, and, often, opposite things."[22] Yet Hawthorne's mind was not of a temper to bow blithely to this condition any more than was James's. Like *The Sacred Fount*, Hawthorne's last novel undermines the very freewheeling mental activity that it seems to encourage.

There is, of course, ground for contention here. Many readers have felt that once Hawthorne perceived the new freedom offered by an unchecked analogy, he fell victim to it. Speaking of Hawthorne's tendency to intrude upon his narrative and break the illusion, F. O. Matthiessen states, "These convulsive outbreaks of Hawthorne's fancy might be attributed to the fact that he felt such an irresistible compulsion to look for correspondences that he could not check himself even when he turned up bad ones."[23] If analogy were unchecked in *The Marble Faun,* we would have an undefined structure, "stretching into an interminable perspective" to borrow a phrase used to describe St. Peter's basilica. But both the sprawling structure of the basilica and that of the book offer something more:

> Within its vast limits, she thought, and beneath the sweep of its great dome, there should be space for all forms of Christian truth; room both for the faithful and the heretic to kneel; due help for every creature's spiritual want.
>
> . . . Her preconception of St. Peter's was a structure of no definite outline, misty in its architecture, dim and gray and huge, stretching into an interminable perspective, and overarched by a dome like a cloudy firmament. Beneath that vast breadth and height, as she had fancied them, the personal man might feel his littleness and the soul triumph in its immensity. So, in her earlier visits, when the compassed splendor of the actual interior glowed before her eyes, she had profanely called it a great prettiness, a gay piece of cabinet work, on a Titanic scale, a jewel casket, marvelously magnified.
>
> . . . The magic transformation from the minute to the vast has not been so cunningly effected but that the rich adornment still counteracts the impression of space and loftiness. The spectator is more sensible of its limits than of its extent. . . . Besides, such as the church is, it can nowhere be made visible at one glance. It stands in its own way. You see an aisle, or a transept; you see the nave or the tribune; but, on account of its ponderous piers and other obstructions, it is only by this fragmentary process that you get an idea of the cathedral.
>
> There is no answering such objections. The great church smiles calmly upon its critics, and, for all response, says, "Look at me!" and if you still murmur for the loss of your shadowy perspective, there comes no reply, save, "Look at me!" in endless repetition, as the one thing to be said. And, after looking many times, with long intervals in between, you discover that the cathedral has gradually extended itself over the whole compass of your idea; it covers all the site of your visionary temple, and has room for its cloudy pinnacles beneath the dome. (348-50)

These passages provide a metaphorical rendition of the reader's response to the book. Substituting the word *book* for *church* in each of the paragraphs above, one arrives at a fairly complete statement of the critical problems facing the reader of *The Marble Faun*. Our first reaction to the book is like Hilda's to the cathedral. Trying to grasp it as a whole, we have the impression that the ideas it sets forth stretch into an interminable perspective and that since no definite shape or outline seems evident, the work is sufficiently multifaceted to be all things to all readers. Similarly, we find it difficult to move from the minute particularity of the discussions in the work to its larger ideas, to see what it is that joins them, to understand how the realistic detail is part of the larger design and not just superficial adornment. As spectators, we become enmeshed in the detail (a good example is the trouble readers have had with the guidebooklike description), and we conclude that this element only reveals the book's limitations, contributing little or nothing to its conception on the grand scale.

The passage beginning "Besides, such as the church is . . ." forms a succinct statement of the difficulties we encounter if we attempt to explicate the book in terms of an overall structural motif or central theme. Like the church, the book thwarts such visions: "It stands in its own way." We are allowed only fragmentary glimpses of its meaning and are forced to juxtapose these in our own minds to arrive at some sense of its wholeness. Yet, despite all these difficulties, we cannot easily abandon the work or our attempts to perceive even its fragmentary beauties. The book contains the same haunting qualities that Poe's *Pym* and James's *Fount* possess. As in these two books, "The suggestive faculty is tormented rather than genially excited, and in the end is left a prey to doubts."[24] Once caught, however, the interested reader returns to the book again and again for one more look. Like the "one observer in a thousand" who views Kenyon's unfinished bust of Donatello, the reader suspects that the book holds something more: "Most spectators mistake it for an unsuccessful attempt towards copying the features of the Faun of Praxiteles. One observer in a thousand is conscious of something more, and lingers long over this mysterious face, departing from it reluctantly, and with many a glance thrown backward" (381).

This description of the effect the basilica has on an observer is a metaphorical rendition of the perception process that the book itself seeks to effect in the reader. At the first stage of perception, the reader confronts a structure that includes a range of meaning wide enough to represent all things to all people. However, this first impulse is checked; a counterforce is set up by the rich adornment of detail. The structure works against an all-encompassing abstraction of meaning, forcing the perceiver to accept a fragmented view of the whole by calling attention to the limits it imposes. Finally, it allows a new kind of integrated view, one very different from the first in that it possesses a concreteness that can now contain the first vague and misty vision beneath its dome.

* * *

Architectural and sculptural images predominate in *The Marble Faun*.[25] For Hawthorne's last work aims at a formal structure that approximates verbal sculpture. He struggled here to create an aesthetic that will incorporate both the freedom of analogy, a motion-filled play of the imagination, and the repose that will contain this play. Fixity and play are joined in its title in the linking of marble and faun, and it is the same unlikely conjunction of motion-in-stillness that characterizes all the sculpture described in the book. In chapter 2, "The Faun," Kenyon objects because "The Dying Gladiator" never dies: "Flitting moments—imminent emergencies—imperceptible intervals between two breaths—ought not to be incrusted with the eternal repose of marble; in any sculptural subject, there should be a moral standstill, since there must of necessity be a physical one" (16). Similarly, the Laocoön's effect is a result of its containing both elements in an integrated formal structure: "What he most admired was the strange calmness diffused through this bitter strife; so that it resembled the rage of the sea made calm by its immensity, or the tumult of Niagara which ceases to be tumult because it lasts forever" (391).

In terms of the element of play, Hawthorne has been charged with succumbing to an unchecked analogy. On the other hand, the element of fixity draws down upon him another charge. The only brake on analogy at his disposal, critics like Feidelson claim, is an outworn allegory. Discussing Hawthorne's retreat from the implications of a symbolism that "fascinated and horrified him," Feidelson says that Hawthorne fell "back on the simple morality of Hilda, a purely allegorical creature equipped with white robe, tower, lamp, and doves."[26] Hawthorne's analogies do not stop with Hilda at the allegorical level. Like Edwards before him, Hawthorne was seeking to rehabilitate an old form of typology in a new context. The moral fixity, or better, the moral repose in his fiction resides beyond Hilda, at a higher level reached by means of his allusions, the substance of which he invites and expects his reader to provide.

Let us turn first, however, to the element of play. It is hardly less demanding; the reader himself must make it possible. He must be one whose sympathies cause him to linger over a work of art, one who is willing to go the last mile with the author. The result is a rhetorical relationship that places great demands upon the reader. The ability of the work to set his mind in motion is essential to the kind of interaction at which the author has aimed. The first title for the book, *Transformation,* which Hawthorne rejected as reminding him too much of "a clown in Harlequin," points toward this rhetorical phenomenon. The reader is asked to engage in a mental exercise that transforms the given facts of the text. In the passage cited above, for example, Kenyon's model of the Faun seems an unsuccessful attempt at copying. But its merit lies in its incompleteness, in what it suggests. It activates the persistent observer's imagination, encouraging him to look beyond the object placed before him. The book, another copy of the Faun, operates in the same way. The passage itself affords an example of the interaction between reader and text. Here, just as Kenyon copies the Faun, Hawthorne has copied Milton. The viewer's and reader's backward glancing is reminiscent of Adam and Eve's departure from the Garden.

The idea of suggestiveness in a work of art is a crucial concept to Hawthorne. It is closely aligned with two other states of being that recur in his fictions and in his critical statements: the idea of an unfinished state and that of the sketch. Whichever of the three terms we choose to apply, it appears repeatedly that good art is art that remains in a state of incompleteness. In *The Italian Notebooks* Hawthorne praised "The Dying Gladiator":

> Like all other works of the highest excellence . . . it makes great demands upon the spectator; he must make a generous gift of his sympathies to the sculptor, and help out his skill with all his heart, or else he will see little more than a skillfully wrought surface. It suggests more than it shows.[27]

This too is the answer of the showman in "Main Street" to the literal-minded heckler who complains that the illusion is not forcible enough to draw him in. He points out that the pasteboard figures of his show must be helped out by the imagination: "Human art has its limits and we must now and then ask a little aid from the spectator's imagination."[28] One of the most explicit statements of the idea occurs in chapter 15 of *The Marble Faun*. At the home of an artist, the four major characters discover a large portfolio of working sketches, supposed to be those of famous artists of the past. The narrative voice comments:

> There is an effluence of divinity in the first sketch; and there, if anywhere, you find the pure light of inspiration, which the subsequent toil of the artist serves to bring out in stronger luster, indeed, but likewise adulterates it with what belongs to an inferior mood. The aroma and fragrance of new thought were perceptible in these designs, after three centuries of wear and tear. The charm lay partly in their very imperfection; for this is suggestive, and sets the imagination at work; whereas the finished picture if a good one, leaves the spectator nothing to do, and, if bad, confuses, stupefies, disenchants, and disheartens him. (138)

The idea of the sketch, of a half-developed form that suggests, is important in Hawthorne's work from the first, but it receives increasing attention in the novels following *The Scarlet Letter,* and, as Roy Harvey Pearce points out, by the time of *The Marble Faun,* "The sketch becomes the very structural core of the romance."[29] Basically, claims Pearce, the sketch is a weakened form of symbolism. It arises when

> received, integrated, localized, firmly grasped values are lost—feeling takes the place of comprehending, grandiosity

> the place of grandeur, pathos the place of understanding, a "Marble Faun" the place of a "Scarlet Letter." The sketches represent, so to speak, a watered-down version of Puritan typology. Emotionality takes the place of specific meaning. Physical states are still representative of spiritual states. . . . But emphasis has been shifted from that spirituality and one's deep humility and self-abasement in the face of it to the satisfying yet "safe" emotional experience which is part of seeing figured in one's surroundings the values by which one has been brought to believe one should live.[30]

Hawthorne produced sketches throughout his working career. The voluminous notebooks, kept through the years, are basically written in this genre. Furthermore, according to Pearce, the sketch plays a more and more decided part in the structure of Hawthorne's novels. In *The Marble Faun,* nine chapters are primarily sketches, serving chiefly "to develop scenic pathos."[31] As a chief example, Pearce cites "Scenes by the Way," a long descriptive chapter of the Italian countryside and country manners.

I would agree almost wholeheartedly with Pearce's evaluation of the sketch genre, but I cannot concur with his intimation that Hawthorne was unaware of its watered-down status. Twice early in *The Marble Faun* the text notes that the heroic has no place here. The image of the Faun itself falls short of the heroic. In chapter 1 we are told, "Perhaps it is the very lack of moral severity, of any high and heroic ingredient in the character of the Faun, that makes it so delightful an object to the human eye and to the frailty of the human heart" (9). The same "lowered" state, achieved by undermining the heroic, is achieved by Miriam in her sketches. The subjects are not at fault. They are proper subjects for heroic treatment. But Miriam finds that in each case she is compelled to add "a certain wayward quirk of her pencil," which undermines the heroic conception and produces something quite different (43).

In the passage about the sketches of the old masters, the language suggests that the sketch represents in art a state of innocence, a beginning that contains "an effluence of divinity" and a certain purity. As the work grows toward a more finished state, it inevitably loses some of this fresh charm. It becomes adulterated and, on another level, in the case of these sketches, suffers the wear and tear of time. Yet it is important not to overlook the fact that the sketch is seen here also as a state of imperfection. The state of the sketch, for all its charm, is not an end to be sought but a beginning. Its imperfection is analogous to the moral imperfection of the untried innocence of the human soul. We are hardly surprised that Hilda is the character most interested in this portfolio. For Hilda too is innocence untried and therefore imperfect. Her sketches are like these: emanating the divine but lacking reality, and hence falling short of good art. Nevertheless, "With years and experience she might be expected to attain a darker and more forcible touch, which would impart to her designs the relief they needed" (55).

If the sketch and its accompanying suggestiveness were seen as the ideal state, an end in itself, we would have to conclude that Hawthorne was of Emerson's camp in this matter. Millicent Bell, as well as she argues for Hawthorne's antiromantic strain in regard to other matters, claims that Hawthorne took the same view as Emerson toward the unfinishedness of all art, that "what a work of art *suggested* was, after all, more significant than what it actually was."[32] For Hawthorne, however, the suggested is more integral to the work, and what is suggested is carefully controlled. One does not find in his work what one finds in Emerson's: an unchecked, untrammeled suggestiveness. Although Hawthorne realized that this kind of unlimited, unchecked expansion was perhaps possible in some remote Golden Age, he saw that art, like humanity, was fallen. If the suggestive sketch is capable of evoking the divine element, a certain sublimity, it was also able by that "wayward quirk of the pencil" to evoke the grotesque and the demonic. In Miriam's sketch of Holofernes and Judith, the severed head "was screwing its eyes upward and twirling its features into a diabolical grin of triumphant malice, which it flung right in Judith's face" (44).

There seems little use in asking when the transgression occurred that makes even the relative innocence of the sketch represent a fallen state. As in *The Scarlet Letter,* Hawthorne is not concerned with a specific sin or the particulars of its commission. Following the tradition of romantic writers, Hawthorne secularized the scriptural event. The Fall is not something that happened only in a single place and time in the mythical past; it is an ongoing act that is repeated in every life and at every possible level of experience. Each of the main characters in *The Marble Faun* recapitulates it to some degree in the course of the story. The history of the counts of Monte Beni traces its effects in terms of man's loss of contact with the natural world; the city of Rome stands as a monument to the fall and ruin of great civilizations; art itself is fallen; the heroic mode has given way to the ironic, and the resulting ambiguity of language touches everything and profanes even the most innocent sketch. Thus, the staircase to Hilda's tower becomes a Jacob's Ladder or a Tower of Babel, a legitimate way to the divine or a misguided effort that ends in the corruption and disunity of language. This attitude toward language is not peculiar to *The Marble Faun* with its emphasis on the fallen nature of all things. While *The Scarlet Letter* concerns the effect upon man of unspoken and unconfessed sin, its title points to the fact that the letter, the language itself, is adulterated.

Hawthorne's writings are filled with scruples about the practice of art and of his own art in particular. Yet his reservations are justified, for his aesthetic practices arose from an exploitation of the lapsed state. It is appropriate, then, that *The Marble Faun* discusses the problem of the Fortunate Fall. If there is any goodness, moral or aesthetic, in Hawthorne's art, its very existence depends upon the fact of the lapsed world. In the preface to the book, Hawthorne outlined the conditions necessary for the writing of romance as he conceived it, lamenting that the nature of America inhibits rather than encourages the art of romance:

> No author, without a trial, can conceive of the difficulty of writing a romance about a country where there is no shadow, no antiquity, no mystery, no picturesque and gloomy wrong, nor anything but a commonplace prosperity, in broad and simple daylight, as is happily the case with my dear native land. It will be very long, I trust, before romance-writers may find congenial and easily handled themes, either in the annals of our stalwart republic, or in any characteristic and probable

> events of our individual lives. Romance and poetry, ivy, lichens, and wallflowers need ruin to make them grow.

The language here seems heavily weighted in terms of a physical atmosphere, evoking the stage props needed to write in the Gothic mode. Yet even in this passage there is a careful blend of the physical and spiritual attributes necessary to romance. The word *shadow* represents both the physical shadow and a moral or psychological shadow. A *picturesque wrong* reveals the same odd mixture of the physical and moral. The doubleness of spiritual and material requirements extends to the last sentence, in which romance and poetry are classed with natural objects (*wallflower* is a name that Hawthorne applied to himself). And the *ruin* that is needed for romance to grow is both physical decay and moral corruption.

We need not conclude that Hawthorne saw America as unspotted and pure. This passage, like the sketches, is marked by the wayward quirk of the pen, which Hawthorne used here to satirize the American habit of seeing the dear native land and its inhabitants as free from all imputations of moral blame. He also poked fun at the attributes that his fellow Americans invoked as evidence of their moral uprightness—economic prosperity and a tolerant and smiling optimism. The satire is gentle and low-key. Even in "The Celestial Railroad" the satirical note is mitigated by the comic note. Nonetheless, the question of American innocence was crucial to the shaping of Hawthorne's aesthetic practice, for it was profoundly difficult to reach an audience by means of an art based on a common state of sinfulness when the majority of that audience conceived of itself as free from and untouched by any such condition. It is safe to say that Hawthorne viewed American society as heretical. Its "evil" lay in its heretical conviction of and confidence in its own innocence. To give a name to this heresy, we can say that Hawthorne discovered himself a displaced person in a society profoundly Pelagian. His orthodoxy in this matter separates his point of view definitively from the character of Hilda, who has often been identified as his final moral arbiter in the book. Hilda's optimism, her confidence in her ability to choose between good and evil, and her emphasis on her own and others' purity make her not Hawthorne's spokesman but a spokesman for the Pelagian point of view.

Pelagius, in opposition to the Augustinian view of nature, asserted that man was born innocent, that he was born into Adam's state before the Fall. We do not inherit Adam's sin, although we become sinners like him when we sin out of our own moral freedom. Paul Tillich has summarized the appeal of this view of nature:

> Pelagius wanted to avoid the idea of hereditary sin. Sin is not a universally tragic necessity, but a matter of freedom. America is very much in favor of this Pelagian idea that every individual can always make a new beginning, that he is able by his individual freedom to make a decision for or against the divine. The tragic element, on the other hand, is very much known in Europe, and is not so near to the heart of Americans. In Europe the negative side of Augustinianism—we could call it existentialism—has emphasized the tragic element and has reduced the ethical zeal and impact that Pelagianism can have.
>
> The function of Christ under these circumstances is a double one: to provide the forgiveness of sins in baptism to those who believe, and to give an example of a sinless life not only by avoiding sins but also by avoiding the occasions of sins through asceticism.[33]

The second and last function of Christ from the Pelagian point of view places us squarely in the situation and attitudes assigned to Hilda in *The Marble Faun*. In the scene, so repellent to the modern reader, in which the "innocent" Hilda shrinks from contact with "sinful" Miriam, Hilda's whole concern is to protect the spotless garment given her at birth, to avoid sin in order that she can die as pure as she was born. Though she recognizes that she has the potential to sin, she does not see herself as in any way sinful:

> If I were one of God's angels, with a nature incapable of stain, and garments that never could be spotted, I would keep ever at your side, and try to lead you upward. But I am a poor, lonely girl, whom God has set here in an evil world, and given her only a white robe, and bid her wear it back to Him, as white as when she put it on. (208)

Hilda maintains this position in regard to Nature on a larger scale. In chapter 18, "On the Edge of a Precipice," Miriam and Hilda argue over the significance of Curtius's plunge into the chasm to save Rome. For Miriam, the chasm is only one of the rents in Nature that reveal its dark underside. She sees Curtius's action as unheroic and mocks the self-conceit implicit in one man's attempt to save all of Rome. Hilda replies that she doubts any such pit exists. If it does, she says, it has its existence only as a result of sins committed by freely operating moral agents who have the alternative choice of bridging over any such chasm by their own "good thoughts and deeds." She concludes,

> It was the guilt of Rome, no doubt, that caused this gulf to open; and Curtius filled it up with his heroic self-sacrifice and patriotism, which was the best virtue that the old Romans knew. Every wrong thing makes the gulf deeper; every right one helps to fill it up. As the evil of Rome was far more than its good, the whole commonwealth finally sank into it, indeed, but of *no original necessity.* (162, italics mine)

Here, again, is Hawthorne's light touch of irony. The young American, like the old Romans she defends, presents in her little speech the best virtue that she knows. Ironically, her virtue is tinged with patriotism, too. Her view of nature is not orthodox but American, and her Pelagianism emerges with full force in her final assertion that Rome fell of "no original necessity." Human sinfulness is an accidental element of human nature, not an essential one, and had the Romans been a little more virtuous, Rome need never have fallen.

The reader may ask why, if Hilda represents here what I claim she represents, Hawthorne did not condemn her more harshly. There are several reasons for this. In general, we can say that it was not Hawthorne's purpose to condemn with a heavy-handed satire the multiple world views he presented but to expose their limitations by a subtle irony. Hilda's limitations, her naive self-conceit and obtuseness, are exposed repeatedly. Her invulnerability rests, in large part, on the distance she maintains between herself and the rest of the world. Although her tower is described as a hermitage, Hilda is no humble hermit. In a conversation with Miriam she says, "A height of some fifty feet above the roofs of Rome gives me all the advantages that I get from fifty miles of distance. The air so exhilarates my spirits, that sometimes I feel half-inclined to attempt a flight from the top of my tower, in the faith that I should float upward" (54). We may interpret this statement as merely another sign of Hawthorne's extravagant admiration for the angelic Hilda. To do so, however, we must ignore the allusion to Christ in the wilderness. The scene evoked by Hilda's seemingly innocent inclination is that of the second temptation:

> Then the devil took him to the holy city, and set him on a pinnacle of the temple, and said to him, "If you are the Son of God, throw yourself down; for it is written, 'He will give his angels charge of you,' and 'On their hands they will bear you up, lest you strike your foot against a stone.' " Jesus said to him, "Again it is written, 'You shall not tempt the Lord your God.' " (Matt. 4:5–7)

Miriam's reply to Hilda—"Oh, pray don't try it! . . . If it should turn out that you are less than an angel, you would find the stones of the Roman pavement very hard; and if an angel, indeed, I am afraid you would never come down among us again" (54)—only obscures the issue. It diverts our attention and makes the issue at stake appear to be whether Hilda is of an angelic nature. The context established by the allusion renders the question grotesque, for as the biblical text makes clear, the question is not about one's nature; it involves the problem of whether one ought to tempt God in an act of spiritual pride.

At the end of the book, the author says he hoped to succeed well enough that no reader would "insist on being told, in so many words, whether [Donatello] had furry ears or no. As respects all who ask such questions, the book is, to that extent, a failure" (464). We can conclude that if the reader who asks "such questions" has missed the central experience offered by the book, then the character who asks—Hilda—has also missed the point of her experience. Again, the context lends a grotesqueness to Hilda's state of mind, for she asks Kenyon when she is agitated, prompted by the sight of a veiled, kneeling figure whom she suspects is Miriam. The question is then followed by Kenyon's description of the great change that has overtaken Donatello. Hilda, we realize, has missed the entire transformation. Having had no encounter with Donatello since the crime was committed, she has been both literally and metaphorically excluded from the central experience of the book.

Yet Hawthorne could no more condemn Hilda than he could the reader who has missed the point of the novel. Hilda and perhaps the reader, too, have time on their side. She is at an early stage in the growth of consciousness, and, like the sketch, her imperfections constitute a part of her charm, once we realize the transitoriness of her state. It is only when we see the point of view represented by Hilda as fixed and unchanging that we consider her a threat. In chapter 41, "Snowdrops and Maidenly Delights," we are again reminded that Hilda's growth lies in the future and that her present state is as ephemeral as spring flowers "that will die while you are handling them, and bequeath you a delicious legacy . . . in the perception of their evanescence and unreality" (374). To recognize this fact about Hilda alters our perception of the book's end. Kenyon and Hilda's departure from Rome echoes as much as Miriam and Donatello's wanderings the departure of Adam and Eve from the Garden. Despite Hilda's hopefulness, the couple is, after all, counting on a life full of "human promise," an existence that will no longer "defer the reality of life" (461). Only if we have come through *The Marble Faun* as unscathed as Hilda can we entertain the naively romantic idea that no woe and pain lie before them.

There are further reasons for the careful treatment of Hilda, however, reasons that lead us to the heart of Hawthorne's aesthetic practices. Poe, exploring the outer limits of art, confronted us with the question of what degree of likeness exists between man as creator and God as creator. Hawthorne also pushed at the boundaries between art and morality, but the concern of his fiction is with the moral efficacy of a work of art. Poe asked to what extent the artist is God-like; Hawthorne asked how far he is Christ-like. Or, to state the problem in another way, how can art that is fallen save itself and become once again a means of redemption for its audience?

Hawthorne of course had to answer in the negative the proposition that art can redeem itself. To assert that it can save itself is to place art in the same realm in which Hilda's Pelagianism places human moral action, a realm of do-it-yourself redemption that denies the need for grace. And art, if once in some sense redemptive, is now decidedly fallen and impotent:

> The love of art, therefore, differs widely in its influence from the love of nature; whereas, if art had not strayed away from its legitimate paths and aims, it ought to soften and sweeten the lives of its worshipers, in even a more exquisite degree than the contemplation of natural objects. But, of its own potency, it has no such effect; and it fails, likewise, in that other test of its moral value which poor Hilda was now involuntarily trying upon it. It cannot comfort the heart in affliction; it grows dim when the shadow is upon us. (340)

Hilda is not the only character to experience the failure of art. Donatello, in the depths of his depression after the crime, tells Kenyon that he is now indifferent to it, that it offers him neither pleasure nor pain. The pretext for Kenyon's alienation from art is even slighter. Disappointed by Hilda's failure to keep her appointment to accompany him in a tour of the Vatican galleries, the "chill of his disappointment" causes him to suspect that his beloved sculpture is a "very cold art" (391).

Significantly, in that state of mind, one work of art still has the power to produce an effect upon him:

> Nothing pleased him, unless it were the group of the Laocoön, which, in its immortal agony, impressed Kenyon as a type of the long fierce struggle of man, involved in the knotted entanglements of Error and Evil, those two snakes, which, if no divine help intervene, will be sure to strangle him and his children in the end. What he most admired was the strange calmness diffused through this bitter strife; so that it resembled the rage of the sea made calm by its immensity, or the tumult of Niagara which ceases to be tumult because it lasts forever. Thus, in the Laocoön, the horror of the moment grew to be the fate of interminable ages. Kenyon looked upon the group as the one triumph of sculpture, creating the repose, which is essential to it, in the very acme of turbulent effort; but, in truth, it was his mood of unwonted despon-

> dency that made him so sensitive to the terrible magnificence, as well as to the sad moral, of this work. (391–92)

The figure of the Laocoön sculpture appears sporadically throughout the book. Metaphorically embedded in the descriptions of it lies, at least partially, Hawthorne's solution to his problem. If art is fallen, how does one restore to it some degree of moral efficacy? Hawthorne's reply is that one begins with the lapsed state of both art and nature and uses art to expose the errors that beset one at every stage of moral growth. Art's function is negative. It serves as a corrective. Because it cannot be positively redemptive in its present state, it must serve morality by revealing the false ideas that contribute to the fallen nature of both art and humanity.

William Bysshe Stein points out in *Hawthorne's Faust: A Study of the Devil Archetype* that the demonic has long been used as an educative principle in Christianity. Hawthorne continued the tradition while extending it to serve his own specific purposes. Because language is fallen and thus partakes of the demonic, it can no longer function to create the heroic mode. Word and object have lost their original primal unity. The word, like human consciousness, has become self-conscious, full of irony and ambiguity. However, this very quality of ambiguity can be used to create a pattern of ironic allusions that point back to models representing and partaking in some measure of the original unity represented by the heroic mode. In short, the instability of language is used to evoke stable models of judgment. In this way Hawthorne attempted to create an aesthetic situation in the medium of language that, like the Laocoön, creates repose in the midst of turbulent effort.

The Faustian contract appears early in *The Marble Faun*. In chapter 3, "Subterranean Reminiscences," we are told that some months before the four principal characters had made an excursion to the catacomb of St. Calixtus. During the course of their tour, Miriam wanders away from the group, and the others fear she will be hopelessly lost in the dark labyrinthine passages. She is guided back to them by, or, it may be, serves as guide to, a man dressed in a costume reminiscent of the satyrs of old. This is Miriam's model, who shadows her until

Donatello kills him by flinging him over the precipice. Several interpretations of her adventure in the catacombs are circulated in the community, and Miriam herself offers several fantastic explanations of the event to Kenyon and Hilda. On one occasion, she tells them that the specter has offered to teach her a long-forgotten technique for fresco painting. On her side, all she must do is agree to accompany him back to the catacombs. Here the narrative voice is unreliable, ironically pretending to concur with the idea that the Faustian contract is irresistible to the artist: "And what true votary of art would not purchase unrivaled excellence, even at so vast a sacrifice!" (34).

Even more to the point is Miriam's second explanation of the incident. The model is an infidel, and

> she had entered into controversy with him, hoping to achieve the glory and satisfaction of converting him to the Christian faith. For the sake of so excellent a result, she had even staked her own salvation against his, binding herself to accompany him back into his penal gloom if, within a twelve-month's space, she should not have convinced him of the errors through which he had so long groped and stumbled. (34)

If there is any basis for the claim that Hilda represents one aspect of Hawthorne's mind, an equal claim may be made that Hawthorne enacts as well the role of the specter. In his fictions, and especially in *The Marble Faun,* he plays devil's advocate. The book is full of heretical positions, like Hilda's Pelagianism, which the reader is invited to correct. Or, if the reader himself holds one of these points of view, the text ironically undercuts and exposes the errors of that position. Whether the reader converts, transforms the text, or the text the reader, is not made entirely clear. In Miriam's story it is she who "saves" or attempts to save the specter. Earlier, Hilda says that Providence has rescued Miriam from the darkness. Miriam replies, "Are you quite sure that it was Heaven's guidance which brought me back? If so, it was by an odd messenger, as you will confess" (29). Both the transaction and the agent of the transaction are treated with a shadowy ambivalence, but one thing is clear—the movement is from darkness to light, from error or heresy to a more correct view of man's nature.

Before leaving the subject of heresy, of art that is slightly askew due to a wayward quirk of the pen, I would invite the reader to recall the well-known passage in "The Custom-House" in which Hawthorne speaks of his Puritan ancestors. He places in their mouths a speech condemning his vocation as a writer: "A writer of story-books! What kind of a business in life—what mode of glorifying God, or being serviceable to mankind in his day and generation—may that be? Why, the degenerate fellow might as well have been a fiddler!"[34] His only reply to their charge is, "And yet, let them scorn me as they will, strong traits of their nature have intertwined themselves with mine." What traits, we may ask, did Hawthorne see himself as sharing with these men? If we read the entire passage carefully, the one trait that presents itself as hereditary is the spirit of persecution. The first father is a "bitter persecutor"; "his son, too, inherited the persecuting spirit."[35] If the last of a long line of persecutors of heresy, Hawthorne proves to be, as in the case of Hilda, the gentlest. The appeal of the statue of the Marble Faun and of the book modeled after it "is the very lack of moral severity"; nor does it possess "an atom of martyr's stuff in all that softened marble" (16). The martyr's role was rejected by Hawthorne because it comes dangerously close to the heresy he pursued. It assumes that a fallen nature can redeem itself and others. In "The Custom-House" passage he goes on to mock his own pretentions to the role of "redeemer" of his race:

> At all events, I, the present writer, as their representative, hereby take shame upon myself for their sakes, and pray that any curse incurred by them—as I have heard, and as the dreary and unprosperous condition of the race, for many a long year back, would argue to exist—may be now and henceforth removed.[36]

In the preceding discussion, the emphasis on the limitations of this aesthetic must make it seem ineffective, a true product of the mind of the "harmless Hawthorne." Yet Hawthorne's scruples are justified. He too is using an odd messenger to alter the consciousness of his readers. If he fails to convert their minds—that is, if he introduces them to the ironic mode and does not point them beyond it—he has only replaced untroubled innocence with a darker, more despairing vision. And if that is the result, he is left to face the question, later posed by James's narrator, of what value lies in forcing people to crack and split from within. In short, what good is there in destroying the psychic unity of an innocent mind if one can only replace it with a disintegrated state and not move to a third and higher form of unified consciousness? The aesthetic implications echo this dilemma. In Miriam's account of the specter, she tells Kenyon and Hilda that she is not winning the battle to convert the man-demon; having capitulated to him, "she must take an eternal farewell of the sun!" (34). Similarly, if Hawthorne failed to create a form that moves beyond irony, the practice of his art must result in a nihilistic and absurd vision devoid of all elements of realism and of hope.

If Hawthorne possessed the ideal audience that he addresses with longing in preface after preface, there would hardly be cause for concern. Ideally, the fictional transaction would carry the reader from a state of innocence into the darkness and out again to a state of greater self-knowledge and moral maturity. But what if, in this reenactment of the Fall, the third stage of the life-death-resurrection cycle fails? What if the reader, on discovering that sin, evil, the demonic lies within—either within himself or within the fictional transaction to which he has in all good faith and trust surrendered himself—becomes caught like the figures in the Laocoön in the second stage of the revelation? The possibility is explored allegorically in "Young Goodman Brown." The revelation of sin within himself and in those whom he trusts destroys Brown's innocence and leaves him nothing with which to replace it. His final state of morbidity is like that which Kenyon sees in Donatello at Monte Beni. He tells his despondent friend:

> Believe me, you know not what is requisite for your spiritual growth, seeking, as you do, to keep your soul perpetually in the unwholesome region of remorse. It was needful for you to pass through that dark valley, but it is infinitely dangerous to

> linger there too long; there is poison in the atmosphere, when we sit down and brood in it, instead of girding up our loins to press onward. (273)

At this point in the book, Kenyon's theology is askew. He takes up Hilda's position that the solution to Donatello's problem is a renewed moral effort, that good works can extricate him from his predicament. But if the solution he offers is wrong, his perception of the situation is more right than perhaps even he knows. Modeling Donatello's bust, he creates an expression of Donatello's features at the moment of the murder. He refuses to leave the work in that state because, as he tells Donatello, "It were a sin to let the clay which bears your features harden into a look like that" (272).

The same danger of capitulating to the demonic is symbolically enacted in "The Birthmark." An already beautiful woman submits to an experiment intended to remove the flaw in her beauty. Significantly, her only imperfection is a birthmark, perhaps symbolic of the state of sin in which she was born. She admires her husband's idealism, his love that "would accept nothing less than perfection nor miserably make itself contented with an earthier nature than he had dreamed of."[37] The attempt to render her more perfect on the part of her scientist husband leads to her destruction. The story ends with her death and the gross, hoarse laughter of the scientist's demonic assistant.

Hawthorne knew only too well how much he lacked an ideal reader. Viewing the situation realistically, he realized his audience was predominantly made up of fictional Hildas, of real-life Sophias. For them as for Young Goodman Brown there was always the possibility that they could only come to grief in his fictional world. In a world of "sin, care and self-consciousness," as Kenyon says, "the simplest character is ever the soonest to go astray" (239–40). I have argued that our judgment of Hilda must be ameliorated because she has time on her side, that experience will change her. Yet there is a sense in which Hilda will never change. Experience may render her judgments more sober and somewhat chasten her optimism, but the radical change, the transformation to a point of view that can encompass the demonic and absurd, is beyond her. For Hilda's nature is of the type that William James was later to describe in *The Varieties of Religious Experience* as the once-born personality. James noted that this kind of personality has had powerful influence in anti-Christian movements as well as within Christianity: "They owed their influence to a certain authoritativeness in their feeling that Nature, if you will trust her sufficiently, is absolutely good." Furthermore,

> It is to be hoped that we all have some friend, perhaps more often feminine than masculine, and young than old, whose soul is of this sky-blue tint, whose affinities are rather with birds and flowers and all enchanting innocencies than with dark human passions, who can think no ill of man or God, and in whom religious gladness, being in possession from the outset, needs no deliverance from any antecedent burden.[38]

James's work borrows its terminology directly from Francis W. Newman, who is quoted below. The passage is worth reproducing for the light it throws on the character of Hilda:

> God has two families of children on this earth, *the once-born* and *the twice-born*. . . . [The once-born] see God, not as a strict Judge, not as a Glorious Potentate; but as the animating Spirit of a beautiful harmonious world, Beneficent and Kind, Merciful as well as Pure. The same characters generally have no metaphysical tendencies: they do not look back into themselves. Hence they are not distressed by their own imperfections: yet it would be absurd to call them self-righteous; for they hardly think of themselves *at all*. This childlike quality of their nature makes the opening of religion very happy to them: for they no more shrink from God, than a child from an emperor, before whom the parent trembles: in fact, they have no vivid conception of *any* of the qualities in which the severer Majesty of God consists. He is to them the impersonation of Kindness and Beauty. They read his character, not in the disordered world of man, but in romantic and harmonious nature. Of human sin they know perhaps little in their own hearts and not very much in the world; and human suffering does but melt them to tenderness. Thus, when they approach God, no inward disturbance ensues; and without being as yet spiritual, they have a certain complacency and perhaps romantic sense of excitement in their simple worship.[39]

Although James could hope that we all have some friend like this, he knew that such personalities also have a dark side. They are often tyrannical in their efforts to prevent any expression of a point of view that contradicts their own optimism. Hilda repeatedly refuses to give Miriam or Kenyon a hearing. When Kenyon suggests that sin has a very real existence and function in the world, Hilda cries, "Oh, hush! This is terrible and I could weep for you, if you indeed believe it. Do not you perceive what a mockery your creed makes, not only of all religious sentiments, but of moral law—and how it annuls and obliterates whatever precepts of Heaven are written deepest within us? You have shocked me beyond words" (460). Hilda is, as usual, wrong here, egotistically assuming that her view of religious experience is equated with happiness. Nor does it mock moral law, only the rigid black-and-white dicta that Hilda equates with moral law. She is right, however, in her perception that a recognition of evil, of the disorder in the world, is capable of annulling and obliterating religion as she conceives it.

Hawthorne could neither write a "sunshiny" book for the Hildas in his world nor assume that his own view of human nature gave him the right to meddle with the organization of their personalities, to attempt to perfect natures that if blemished possessed their own special charm. To protect them and to be true, at the same time, to his own vision, he was forced to weave his own point of view deep within the texture of his fictions. This fact more than any other accounts for the safeguards in Hawthorne's fiction, the deeply veiled quality of all his work.

The stages of moral transformation presented in *The Marble Faun,* the movement from life or innocence to death and to a resurrection or state of redemption, are paralleled by three states of aesthetic perception. From Hilda's point of view, reality contains no elements that blur into one another. She rejects the idea of a faun, a creature who partakes of both human and animal natures. There is no ambiguity in her world. Correspondingly, the Hilda-reader confronts the text as a series of dichotomies about which he must make an either-or decision and ignore the ambivalence and absurdity that the story contains. But if we move beyond Hilda's position, we find ourselves in the state of confused ambivalence that predominates in the middle of the book. This second stage of moral and aesthetic perception is represented by Donatello in the depths of his remorse, and his confusion finds its parallel in the reader. Donatello tells Kenyon, "You stir up many thoughts but the multitude and whirl of them make me dizzy" (273), and, later, Kenyon himself will be reduced to a similar state of mind. Depressed over Hilda's disappearance, Kenyon moves through the carnival, seeking the one clue that will give meaning to the absurdity that surrounds him. The narrative voice tells us:

> The old Englishman and his daughters, in the opposite balcony, must have seen something unutterably absurd in the sculptor's deportment, poring into this whirlpool of nonsense so earnestly, in quest of what was to make his life dark or bright. Earnest people, who try to get a reality out of human existence, are necessarily absurd in the view of the revelers and masqueraders. (450)

Earnest readers, too, poring over this absurd and nonsensical text in an attempt to wrench some meaning from it, have felt not a little foolish.

Much as we are tempted to assign the work to the category of exercises in absurdity, we are tantalized by the intimations that it holds something more. It does seem impossible to hold in our minds and give order to the manifold associations evoked by innumerable references to both mythical and historical figures and events. Nor does it seem likely that we can reconcile the endless dichotomies presented. Yet a promise of some kind of reconciliation between all the elements whose relationships have been subverted by the Fall is always held out to us. Despite St. Peter's cathedral being structured to stand in its own way and preventing a coherent view of its wholeness, we are told that we can reach a point of view that will allow us to sense its all-encompassing greatness. In the description of the unfinished bust of the Faun, we are warned that the unfinished appearance is a mask pointing to a higher state of moral development, to something beyond itself.

Part of our problem in moving from the second stage of perception to a third and higher one, from absurdity to some form of reconciliation, stems from the book itself, which provides no model among the characters of the final stage of moral growth or aesthetic perception. The text is unfinished in this sense and, true to Hawthorne's dictum, leaves the reader with plenty to do. Like Kenyon, we are left staring into a whirlpool of nonsense, hoping to find the clue or thread that will lead us out of the labyrinth. The narrative voice suggests in the central chapter of the book, "Sunshine," that a model does exist, but offers us little hope in finding it:

> Donatello made no answer, but sat awhile, appearing to follow with his eyes one of the figures, which was repeated many times over in the groups upon the walls and ceiling. It formed the principal link of an allegory, by which (as is often the case in such pictorial designs) the whole series of frescoes were bound together, but which it would be impossible, or, at least, very wearisome, to unravel. The sculptor's eyes took a similar direction, and soon began to trace through the vicissitudes—once gay, now somber—in which the old artist had involved it, the same individual figure. He fancied a resemblance in it to Donatello himself. (227)

The central, binding figure of the book has often been identified as Donatello, but in fact we never see Donatello in his last stage of transformation. From the moment of his reconciliation with Miriam, we see him masked or in disguise. At the end of the story, it is speculated that he lies somewhere in a dungeon-prison below the ground. Donatello's condition is emblematic of the final stage of perception that the text offers. In order to perceive any kind of coherence, we are forced to move underground, to read as we read in the Poe and James novels, well below the surface of the text. Again, the given text becomes a vehicle, a kind of framework from which to perform the transactions necessary to achieve the final point of view offered.

* * *

Donatello is the figure whose vicissitudes bind the story together on the surface, but he is not the figure who links the fragmented elements (a series of frescoes) of the text. The story begins and ends with a discussion of Donatello's nature. In the opening chapters, Kenyon, Miriam, and Hilda are struck by the resemblance between Donatello and Praxiteles' statue of the Faun. What if Donatello, they conjecture, is a modern incarnation of the true Faun? If he were, then he would form the reconciling link between man and nature in its lower, animal forms. He would be "neither man nor animal, and yet no monster, but a being in whom both races meet on friendly ground" (17). Or, as Miriam expresses it, "You see how this peculiarity defines the position of the Faun; and while putting him where he cannot exactly assert his brotherhood, still disposes us kindly towards the kindred creature. He is not supernatural, but just on the verge of nature, and yet within it" (13). Kenyon replies, "Nature needed, and still needs, this beautiful creature; standing betwixt man and animal, sympathizing with each, comprehending the speech of either race, and interpreting the whole existence of one to the other." The whole discussion makes Hilda uneasy. She wants to hear nothing of any creature that possesses a double nature or who might stand as a needed reconciler between man and nature. Hilda, of course, given her Pelagian view of human nature, requires neither reconciler nor redeemer. As her friends put the matter, she "has no need of mercy." Hilda believes she can save herself from evil. She is, in effect, her own redeemer.

There is a further reason for Hilda's discomfort at these speculations. The discussion is representative of a technique of displacement that permeates the book and gives a dual nature to the text, enabling it to be both profoundly serious and grotesquely comic. In this particular instance, the conversation is a comic inversion of a discussion of Christ's nature. Kenyon, later in the book, fancies that Donatello resembles the central figure in the allegory. The figure evoked or pointed to in the allusions *is* Christ and the fact of the Christian incarnation. Donatello only *resembles* the figure, and the resemblance is always slightly askew, never one of strict identification. If the reader holds in mind this model while reading the passages cited above, an element of the ludicrous emerges. Miriam's remarks become comically patronizing. From the viewpoint of Christian orthodoxy, Christ's incarnation healed the breach created by Adam's fall and reconciled man with the divine and the natural world. In light of this, Kenyon's solemn speculation that "nature needed, and still needs" a go-between is irrelevant and naively irreverent. I have used Frye's term *displacement* to describe this technique merely for lack of a better one. One might call the effect parodic except that parody usually works in the opposite direction, a nonsensical or absurd text being used to render comic a more serious work. In this case, the reader is expected to hold up a more serious work or more orthodox idea to render comic or to expose the limitations of the text before him. Let us turn for examples to one of the serious models evoked repeatedly in the text, Dante's *Divine Comedy.*

In chapter 7, entitled "Beatrice," there is no overt mention of Dante's Beatrice. The topic of conversation between Miriam and Hilda is Beatrice Cenci, whose portrait Hilda is recreating from memory. In the course of the discussion, the two women, guided by Hilda's "judgment," conclude that Beatrice's crime was inexpiable and that she is beyond all grace and mercy. Ironically, the chapter ends with the talk turning to the Virgin, a figure of merciful compassion. This concluding irony is matched by the opening sentences of the chapter in which the theologically misguided Hilda is extolled as the perfect guide through the art galleries of Rome: "Happy were those (but they were very few) whom she ever chose to be the companions of her day; they saw the art treasures of Rome under her guidance, as they had never seen them before. Not that Hilda could dissertate or talk learnedly about pictures; she would probably have been puzzled by the technical terms of her own art" (62). Hilda does enrich her companions' perceptions by means of her perfect sympathy, and Kenyon the artist may be very happy for her companionship. Yet set beside Dante and his guide, Beatrice, who is capable not only of correcting his misapprehensions of divine law but of leading him to a final and beatific vision, Hilda becomes a touchingly pathetic and slightly absurd substitute.

A similar evocation of Dante's work occurs in chapter 19, "The Faun's Transformation." In the immediate aftermath of their crime, Miriam and Donatello attempt to envision themselves as romantic renegades beyond good and evil. Their first impulse is to rejoice in the new union and sympathy that exists between them. As Miriam says, "The deed knots us together, for time and eternity, like the coil of a serpent" (174). The narrative voice expands on her comment, "Their deed—the crime which Donatello wrought, and Miriam accepted on the instant—had wreathed itself, as she said, like a serpent, in inextricable links about both their souls, and drew them into one, by its terrible contractile power. It was closer than a marriage bond." Any idea of romantic rebellion that may exist in the reader's mind, however, is undercut by the suggestion given here of the twenty-fifth canto of *The Inferno*. That canto, like this chapter, is concerned with transformation; the most perverse and revolting imagery of *The Inferno* is used to describe the metamorphosis, by means of snakes embracing men, from man to beast to man. To call to mind this canto casts a chill, white light of horror on this union and over the otherwise innocuous fact of Donatello's supposed half-man, half-animal nature. A tragic note is added as well by Donatello's claim that they "are cemented with [the specter's] blood," since the phrase is a figure of speech used to describe the union of all Christians, cemented together by the blood of Christ.

One further example of the Dante model may be cited before we move on to examine Hawthorne's use of scriptural models. At the end of the story, Kenyon wanders through the carnival scene, seeking Hilda, and is made the subject of a "merry martyrdom." In the course of his dreamlike ordeal, he witnesses a grand procession consisting of military escorts and gorgeous coaches: "By the old-fashioned magnificence of this procession, it might worthily have included his Holiness in person, with a suite of attendant Cardinals, if those sacred dignitaries would kindly have lent their aid to heighten the frolic of the Carnival" (442–43). Once again, the picture of Kenyon presented here is slightly askew, a grotesque and "fallen" version of the model it evokes. Dante, the pilgrim, undergoes humiliation at the end of his journey through purgatory and is rewarded with a vision of the Church in its redeemed state just before he is reunited with Beatrice. The procession Dante sees is described in military terms, for the Church militant has triumphed over both the secular state and the degenerate Church of Dante's own time. The fallen quality of the vision given Kenyon is heightened by the model. At first, Kenyon believes the procession a religious one, even if consisting only of figures of the corrupt, worldly officialdom of the Roman Church. Yet even that vision proves too much to hope for, an illusion. Viewed more closely, it reveals itself as a procession representative of civil authority: "But, for all its show of a martial escort, and its antique splendor of costume, it was but a train of the municipal authorities of Rome—illusive shadows, every one, and among them a phantom, styled the Roman Senator—proceeding to the Capitol." The world is indeed fallen. Hawthorne's use of *The Divine Comedy* and *Paradise Lost* throughout the text creates a displacement that emphasizes the degraded state of the external world, especially the world of art. Hilda has replaced Beatrice, and an absurd vision has replaced Dante's beatific vision.

In Hawthorne's view, however, evil lies both outside oneself, in the external world, and in the human heart. For this reason, his most pervasive model for displacement is scriptural language and an orthodox Christian viewpoint. The language of the text, by means of subtle suggestions and allusions, invites the reader to bring forward models that throw into sharp focus the otherwise dim and confusing moral positions occupied by the characters. The characters' perceptions are presented repeatedly as slightly askew. Their inner confusion or sin lies in mistaken assumptions about the means and object of redemption, a misdirection of will and understanding that is given an emblematic form at the end of the book in a scene between Kenyon and Hilda. Touring the Pantheon, they approach a shrine in order to see if they can make any sense of the dusky picture hanging behind the altar. The picture proves "little worth looking at," but their attention is caught by the presence of a plump cat complacently sunning herself on the altar. "Their footsteps disturbing her, she awoke, raised herself, and sat blinking in the sun, yet with a certain dignity and self-possession, as if conscious of representing a saint" (458). Kenyon makes a joke of the cat setting herself up "as an object of worship." Ironically, Hilda enjoins Kenyon to help her remove the cat, saying, "It distresses me to see that poor man [a peasant kneeling before the shrine], or any human being, directing his prayers so much amiss."

The irony, of course, is all for the reader. For at this point, the reader ought to have realized that the dusky pictures that make up the book are a pretext for drawing him in and then diverting his attention to both the problems raised and the humor provided by the setting up of false images of worship. Kenyon and Hilda can agree that a cat has no place on the altar, yet they are blind to their own culpable tendencies to replace true objects of worship with false ones. Hilda worships purity for its own sake. Kenyon, winning Hilda at the end of the story, mistakenly looks to her for salvation, as the one who can take him "home." We are told that "Hilda was coming down from her old tower, to be herself enshrined and worshipped as a household saint, in the light of her husband's fireside" (461). They have decided to return to America, the narrative voice continues, because life was now so full of "*human* promise" (italics mine). Kenyon seems to have forgotten, or perhaps never did give significance to his perception of, the smile on Hilda's face at the moment of her resurrection, her reemergence into society. "That soft mirthful smile caused her to melt, as it were, into the wild frolic of the Carnival, and become not so strange and alien to the scene as her unexpected apparition must otherwise have made her" (451). Hilda enshrined is only another absurdity, another facet of the Carnival. The discovery awaits the two, another Adam and Eve, as they set out to make a new home for themselves in America. Inadvertently, Hilda may assume the role of Beatrice. The discovery of her limitations, both on her part and on Kenyon's, may serve to point, as Beatrice does, beyond herself to the true objects of spiritual faith and love.

The text itself functions in this way. It exposes its own limitations, its own state of displacement through the use of allusions, and so points always beyond itself. It is this phenomenon that gives it a quality of inconclusiveness. A mental transaction is initiated by the text, but it is left to the reader to complete it. We have already seen how the refocusing process works in the discussion of Donatello's nature, in Hilda's imaginary flight from the tower, and in the Dante models. Let us turn briefly to the text for a few final examples of the way in which the reader is led to transform the text in the process of filling up the spiritual lacunae it creates.

After the discussion of Curtius's death and the efficacy of good works in compensating for evil in the world, Kenyon speculates that the chasm is full of "all the blood that the Romans shed, whether on battlefields, or in the Coliseum, or on the cross" (163). The two final and specific deaths he cites are those of Caesar and of Virginia, "that pure little rivulet from Virginia's bosom, too! Virginia, beyond all question, was stabbed by her father, precisely where we are standing." Hilda replies, "Then the spot is hallowed forever!" And Miriam asks, "Is there such blessed potency in bloodshed?"—and quickly adds, "Nay, Hilda, do not protest! I take your meaning rightly." A kind of graduated missing of the mark occurs here. Miriam turns the question into a jest that all bloodshed, both murder and martyrdom, is equally blessed and efficacious. Hilda's interpretation, which Miriam claims she does grasp, focuses on the sacrifice of Virginia—a sacrificial death that results from the need to preserve Virginia's purity—and reveals again Hilda's preoccupation with the subject. Though both women have just discussed how evil is atoned for in the world, they appear naively blind to the suggestion that redemption results from Christ's death on the cross.

The same blindness to the redemptive act is exhibited by Kenyon in counseling Donatello on how to escape from his burden of guilt. Kenyon argues that Donatello must not try to save himself by entering a monastery; he should instead perform good works in the world at large. Kenyon casts his argument in terms of the Roman Catholic solution versus the Protestant solution. As a Protestant, he says, with an insupportable burden and needing to make "a peace-offering towards Heaven—I would make the wide-world my cell, and good deeds to mankind my prayer" (195). Donatello replies, "Ah, but you are a heretic!" Although Donatello's remark is directed at Kenyon's *Protestant* solution to the problem of guilt, it has implications much broader than either Kenyon or Donatello can imagine. Kenyon's heresy lies in his assertion that good works are the means of redemption, a doctrine that neither Catholics nor Protestants accept. His ignorance of grace gives a ludicrous air to his heated argument over the respective merits of contemplative works versus works of action. A similar lacuna exists in Miriam's speculations about the doctrine of the Fortunate Fall. The fortunate aspect of the Fall, as celebrated in the Mass, is that it occasioned Christ's redemption of man and history—all of which Miriam ignores while extolling the good that results from man's acquaintance with evil. Her speech is pathetic. The Fall of Man is, as she says, repeated in the romance of Monte Beni, and, ironically, she recapitulates it here with her Eve-like argument that the fruit of sin will make man know good and evil and raise him to a higher level of existence.

Donatello's fall has robbed him of his innocence, but there is no evidence that it has redeemed him or Miriam. Externally, his fall is his act of murdering the specter; inwardly it consists of his naive assumption that he can save Miriam from the shadow thrown over her soul. Early in the story, Donatello's relationship to Miriam is cast in terms of a faithful discipleship. He tells her that he has no other path in life but to follow her. But his discipleship ends in grief for both of them because neither is able to keep devotion within proper bounds. Just before the murder takes place, Miriam invites Donatello to join her in drinking from the Fountain of Trevi. He replies, "Signorina, what you drink, I drink" (144). In Matt. 20:22 and Mark 10:38, the disciples James and John ask Jesus to guarantee them places of prominence nearly equal to his own when he comes into his glory. Jesus tells them, "You know not what you ask: can you drink of the cup that I drink of?" Unwittingly, the two disciples in their hubris and naïveté have asked for martyrdom and later receive it, dying by crucifixion. Donatello's martyrdom is of a lesser kind and, in terms of its inefficacy, is almost meaningless. He will spend his life languishing in prison. The book, by means of multiple allusions, points again and again to the image of Christ and to Nature redeemed. Miriam is doomed to a grotesque inversion of this point of view, "to behold the image of her crime reflected back upon her in a thousand ways, and converting the great, calm face of Nature, in the whole, and in its innumerable details, into a manifold reminiscence of that one dead visage" (190).

There are many more examples that might be cited to illustrate the allusive indirection that permeates the text. I have tried to cite some of the more obvious ones to provide a sense of the imaginative transaction that is required to bring the text to life. Nevertheless, the aesthetic pleasure offered by the book, like the pleasures of the wine of Monte Beni, "eludes analysis" as it suggests a moment of epiphany that "like whatever else is superlatively good . . . was perhaps better appreciated in the memory than by present consciousness" (223). Explaining the allusions in the book is much like attempting to explain a subtle joke or to capture the transitory flavor of the wine: "If you lingered too long upon the draught, it became disenchanted both of its flavor and its fragrance." Finally, the pleasures of the book, like those of the wine, are moral. "Sipping, the guest longed to sip again; but the wine demanded so deliberate a pause, in order to detect the hidden peculiarities and subtile exquisiteness of its flavor, that to drink it was more a moral than a physical enjoyment."

One might justifiably conclude that Hawthorne was well satisfied with this aesthetic. It allowed him to produce a Beatrice-like text, one that avoids the heretical position of being redemptive in and of itself, yet points beyond to spiritual realities and integrated models in which true redemption lies. Nor in the aesthetic transaction is the reader, though placed in a position to redeem the text and capable of making the necessary transformations to bring it to life, allowed to occupy a heretical position. The transaction remains shadowy as it is with Miriam and the specter, for we are never sure which figure in that pair has led the other from darkness back to the light. So too it is difficult to pinpoint cause and effect in the relationship between reader and text. The reader both transforms the text and is acted upon by it to perform these aesthetic transformations. Moreover, the action is redemptive. Early in the book, the narrative voice describes the advantage the sculptor possesses over the poet or writer, an advantage that makes it a nearly priestly obligation for the sculptor to deal with heroic subjects: "His material or instrument, which serves him in the stead of shifting and transitory language, is a pure, white, undecaying substance" (135). The shifting and transitory aspect of language, which is initially seen as its failing, is here, paradoxically, made a virtue. The perverse swings of mood and general instability of the language create a climate in which subtle allusion can operate to effect the transformations described above.

Finally, the aesthetic of *The Marble Faun* conforms to Hawthorne's ideal of Gothic art and architecture. In the series of English essays, *Our Old Home,* written just after *The Marble Faun,* Hawthorne in his descriptions of English cathedrals set forth his criteria for Gothic sublimity. The true Gothic mode incorporates the ridiculous and grotesque: "Methinks it is the test of Gothic sublimity to overpower the Ridiculous without deigning to hide it; and these grotesque monuments of the last century answer a similar purpose with the grinning faces which the old architects scattered among their most solemn conceptions."[40] The Gothic is suggestive, "for there is nothing so fascinating as a Gothic minster, which always invites you deeper and deeper into its heart both by vast revelations and shadowy concealments."[41] As a result, like any good text, it provides multiple levels of meaning:

> The West Front is unspeakably grand and may be read over and over again, forever, and still show undetected meanings, like a great broad page of marvelous writing in black-letter; so many sculptured ornaments there are, blossoming out before your eyes, and gray statues that have grown there since you last looked, and empty niches, and a hundred airy canopies beneath which carved images used to be, and where they will show themselves again, if you gaze long enough.

As in the case of St. Peter's, it is not difficult to make the transition from building to book. *The Marble Faun* possesses a proliferation of meanings, a riot of detail and endless gaps for the imagination to fill. Hawthorne's ambitious attempt at verbal sculpture encompasses the entire city of Rome, the great corpse that the novel seeks to revitalize or resurrect for its readers. But does it succeed? Does it possess the quality of repose essential to the finest sculpture? Psychologically does it create an integrated consciousness or theologically the repose of a state of grace? Most readers conclude that it does not. Hilda, chastened but still a harsh judge, speaks for all those readers and, more important, seems to express Hawthorne's own deepest self-doubts:

> She began to suspect that some, at least, of her venerated painters, had left an inevitable hollowness in their works, because, in the most renowned of them, they essayed to express to the world what they had not in their own souls. . . . They substituted a keen intellectual perception, and a marvellous knack of external arrangement, instead of the live sympathy and sentiment which should have been their inspiration. (338–39)

Some ambivalence must always remain for the reader. The gaps in the text may point to the inevitable hollowness in Hawthorne's work, a confession of his temperamental inability to create a consecrated art or, conversely, to the creation of an aesthetic that, however negatively rendered, conveys the hope of an empty tomb and the act of redemption. To push the matter further, one might argue that there is no dichotomy here, that a gesture of confession is also the first gesture in the process of redemption. Nonetheless, the final structural metaphor presented is sinister. The Pantheon with its great central aperture, an eye gazing toward heaven, evokes for us the transcendental idea of a direct apprehension of the divine and seems to mock Hawthorne's efforts to anchor his endlessly expanding vision in the landscapes that constitute his Eternal City.

In a letter to his publisher, William D. Ticknor, on 6 April 1860, Hawthorne recorded his satisfaction with the book: "But, in fact, if I have written anything well, it should be this Romance; for I have never thought or felt more deeply, or taken more pains."[42] Yet later in that same letter, he acknowledged its odd and limited appeal: "I scarcely thought that these fat-brained Englishmen would have taken so wild a fiction in such good part. To say the truth, some of them do grumble awfully; for it is not every man that knows how to read a Romance, and if I myself were not the author, I doubt whether I would like this one." The writing of romance, by the terms of Hawthorne's definition, was an exercise involving a flirtation with absurdity. During the composition of *The House of the Seven Gables,* he wrote to James T. Fields: "Sometimes, when tired of it, it strikes me that the whole is an absurdity, from beginning to end; but the fact is, in writing a romance, a man is always, or always ought to be, careering on the utmost verge of a precipitous absurdity, and the skill lies in coming as close as possible, without actually tumbling over."[43] As his career progressed, Hawthorne closed rather than widened that gap. Again, in a letter to Fields commenting on the reception of *The Marble Faun,* Hawthorne's words speak far more specifically, and without the reservations of the earlier *Gables* letter, of the role of absurdity in his work: "The book has done better than I thought it would; for you will have discovered, by this time, that it is an audacious attempt to impose a tissue of absurdities upon the public by the mere art of style of narrative."[44]

As James was to recognize in *The Sacred Fount,* Hawthorne realized that the aesthetic of *The Marble Faun* created an oddly imbalanced relationship between form and content. The meaning of the work was embedded in the stylistic gestures rather than in the surface story. The former's ornate and intricate blossoming was only possible by means of a depletion of the story and its characters. Undeniably, style as well as content partakes of meaning in a story, but here, as in the Poe and James works, style bears an inordinate share of the burden. Among some of the more sinister images of *The Marble Faun,* there occurs that of the "parasitical" marriage. In chapter 32, "Scenes by the Wayside," in which, appropriately enough given its title, displacement runs rampant, we encounter the image of grape vines, growing largely untended, that cling to the trees by the roadside. The narrative voice tells us:

> Nothing can be more picturesque than an old grape vine, with almost a trunk of its own, clinging fast around its supporting tree. Nor does the picture lack its moral. You might twist it to more than one grave purpose, as you saw how the knotted, serpentine growth imprisoned within its strong embrace the friend that had supported its tender infancy; and how (as seemingly flexible natures are prone to do) it converted the sturdier tree entirely to its own selfish ends, extending its

> innumerable arms on every bough, and permitting hardly a leaf to sprout except its own. (291–92)

Kenyon, on behalf of his fellow Americans concerned with temperance, sees it as an emblem of the clutching evils of drink. The language of the description, however, the "knotted serpentine" growth, allies this image with that of Laocoön. The embedded pun, "one *grave* purpose," recalls the empty-tomb motif and allows us to see the image as emblematic of the distorted balance between style and content in the work.

Once we are aware of the imbalance, we can understand the litany of concern for the characters that runs through the novel, which opens with a hope that the reader will take an interest in the fortunes of "four individuals." Ironically, the first four individuals to whom we are introduced are the Antinous, the Amazon, the Lycian Apollo, and the Juno. The characters of the book are constantly in danger of losing their lifelikeness and degenerating into mere wooden or stone figures. In fact, they and their story provide a scaffold, a supporting trunk necessary for but of secondary importance to the stylistic transformations that constitute the center of the text. The effect of displacement on the characters is alluded to again in a discussion of how figures from the past compete, so to speak, with the characters of the novel. The historical figures have more reality. The actual figures alluded to are Cicero and Horace, but, of course, the irony rests on the evocation of the historical Christ exposing throughout the characters' foibles and leaving them very "thin," a necessity because we are always looking through them at something beyond:

> It is politic, however, to make few allusions to such a past; nor, if we would create an interest in the characters of our story, is it wise to suggest how Cicero's foot may have stepped on yonder stone, or how Horace was wont to stroll nearby, making his footsteps chime with the measure of the ode that was ringing in his mind. The very ghosts of that massive and stately epoch have so much density that the actual people of today seem the thinner of the two, and stand more

> ghostlike by the arches and columns, letting the rich sculpture be discerned through their ill-compacted substance. (160)

Hawthorne was at home with absurdity, even with absurdity pushed as far as it is in *The Marble Faun,* though he was less easy about its rhetorical effects. He was willing to write out of an aesthetic context in which art was fallen and therefore must rest on the demonic or absurd, to employ an aesthetic that made the artist and his work a guiding Beatrice or a John the Baptist crying in the wilderness. But the justification for that approach was that someone was there to be led, someone to hear the voice and be awakened to love and remorse. Elitism dogged his steps, a single, unwavering disciple. Always conscious of his limited appeal, Hawthorne realized that his last book only seemed to draw the circle tighter. A few weeks before its publication in England, he wrote to Fields: "Possibly I may (or may not) deserve something better than popularity; but looking at all my productions, and especially this latter one, with a cold and critical eye, I can see they do not make their appeal to the popular mind."[45]

The book imposes an inordinate burden on even the not-so-popular mind. Henry James, commenting on the work in his *Hawthorne* in 1879, found it less "simple and complete" than Hawthorne's other novels. The mixing of genres troubled him, but the worst flaw lay in the "art of narration." Moreover, "The story struggles and wanders, is dropped and taken up again, and towards the close lapses into a fatal vagueness."[46] Nonetheless, he saw or felt enough to incorporate many of its themes into his own first novel, *Roderick Hudson.* Perhaps James looked again. No doubt he did so, for nearly twenty years later he ranked *The Marble Faun* among Hawthorne's best work.

To a man who fought against isolation and alienation all his life, the loss of audience was more than an aesthetic problem. Kenyon and Donatello, meditating on the symbolic meaning of stained glass windows, conclude that they represent the glories of heaven, "where a celestial radiance will be inherent in all things and persons, and render each continually transparent to the sight of all" (304). "But," Donatello says, "what a horror it would be if there were a soul among them through which the light could not be transfused!" Kenyon replies,

> Yes, and perhaps this is to be the punishment of sin, not that it shall be made evident to the universe, which can profit nothing by such knowledge, but that it shall insulate the sinner from all sweet society by rendering him impermeable to light, and, therefore, unrecognizable in the abode of heavenly simplicity and truth. Then, what remains for him, but the dreariness of infinite and eternal solitude? (304)

Hawthorne began writing in hopes of opening an intercourse with the world and of effecting some good by means of that intercourse. He must have felt well punished for his excursion away from simplicity into complexity; the world persisted in viewing his radiant stained glass art from the outside, a point of view that made it "nothing better than an incomprehensible obscurity, without a gleam of beauty to induce the beholder to attempt unravelling it" (306). By the end, Hawthorne had lost faith in the moral efficacy of art, no matter how indirect its application. Writing to his sister-in-law, Elizabeth Peabody, he said, "I only know that I have done no good—none whatever."[47] In a letter to Fields (February 1863) he wrote of the recently published series *Our Old Home:* "Heaven sees fit to visit me with an unshakeable conviction that all this series of articles is good for nothing."[48] And one of his last heroes, Septimius Felton, hoping to develop a scheme to save all mankind, only served to illustrate to Hawthorne "the folly of man thinking that he can ever be of any importance to the welfare of the world."[49]

Good was intended even though it took the form of a sugar-coated but bitter pill. Hawthorne sought to hold a dim mirror up to America and his American audience and to show why the heroic was beyond the grasp of American art. Characteristically, he illustrated that the problem was not just external, not just a problem of the American artist lacking physical materials on which to structure his work, but internal as well. The Pelagian view with its optimism about human nature negated tragedy. Hawthorne's own temperamental disinclination to commit himself existentially to the theology that he employed also proved a stumbling block to the creation of art in its highest form. Given these conditions, this American artist's only recourse was to function as a displaced Beatrice, to direct his audience into the darkness of the underworld and out again. Perhaps he received his cue for the role from an early reviewer, or perhaps that reviewer caught a glimpse of Hawthorne's conception of his role in its earliest stage. Lamenting America's lack of a writer of real force, someone with the stature of Milton, Shakespeare, or Homer, Charles Fenno Hoffman wrote in 1838, "Yet men like Hawthorne are not without their use; nay they are the writers to smooth and prepare the path for nobler (but not better) visitants, by softening and ameliorating the public spirit."[50] So we are presented with the "Marble Faun," whose "very lack of moral severity, of any high and heroic ingredient . . . makes it so delightful an object to the human eye and to the frailty of the human heart" (9).

The book catered to its public and at the same time allowed Hawthorne, through displacement and the absurd, to register his own view of human nature. But for Hawthorne, the absurd was a device for preserving sanity in the same limited way that the grotesques in Gothic cathedrals preserved it. He was little inclined to follow Poe into the realm of art in which the absurd predominated. Perhaps he believed that Poe had fully exploited that vein in terms of its American possibilities. In the unfinished *Dr. Grimshawe's Secret,* Hawthorne wrote an aside to himself concerning the course of the plot: "The story must not be founded at all on remorse or secret guilt—all that Poe wore out. Alas me!"[51]

Despite his fears and his growing sense of isolation, Hawthorne, in *The Marble Faun* and the unfinished novels that followed it, pushed his fictions in the direction of the modern novel of the absurd. In each case, he felt he had failed to achieve the particular American form he sought. Final critical judgment may conclude that James succeeded where Hawthorne failed, taking the next step toward modernism, the step that attracted the eye of Gertrude Stein. Yet James had time and distance on his side. And James was not alone: he had Hawthorne as his guide.

Notes

Notes to Introduction

1. Sidney Moss, "*Arthur Gordon Pym* or the Fallacy of Thematic Interpretation," 305.
2. Kenneth Dauber, *Rediscovering Hawthorne*, 21.
3. Tony Tanner, *City of Words: American Fiction 1950–1970*, 21.
4. Charles Feidelson, Jr., *Symbolism and American Literature*, 35.
5. Ibid., 73.
6. For a more complete discussion of the peculiarly American use of analogy, see John F. Lynen, *The Design of the Present*, chapter 1, 29–86.
7. Northrop Frye, *The Anatomy of Criticism*, 136–37.
8. Lynen, *The Design of the Present*, 45–50.
9. Ibid., 49.
10. Tanner, *City of Words*, 27.
11. Richard H. Brodhead, *Hawthorne, Melville, and the Novel*, 115.
12. Arnold P. Hinchcliffe, "Henry James's *The Sacred Fount*," 92.
13. Edgar Allan Poe, *The Complete Works of Edgar Allan Poe*, 13:155. All references to Poe's works are to this 1965 reprint of the 1902 New York edition.
14. Letter quoted in James T. Fields, *Yesterdays with Authors*, 115.
15. Poe, *Complete Works*, 11:108.
16. Henry James, *The Sacred Fount*, 126.

Notes to Chapter I

1. Some representative critics of the positions I outline here: source criticism, Margaret Alterton; psychological criticism, Marie Bonaparte; Allen Tate is a good example of a critic who, while doing Poe justice, nonetheless keeps a careful distance; thematic criticism, D. H. Lawrence. A discussion of Lawrence's essay from *Studies in Classic American Literature* appears later in this chapter.
2. See John T. Irwin, *American Hieroglyphics*, 69. I extend somewhat further here Irwin's claims that Poe's narratives involve "the dissolution of the logical status of discourse." The critical reader confronted by the abyss of Poe's text faces both the dissolution of the logical status of discourse and must contend with language's failure to convey meaning. Perhaps this is because he hasn't the option of the narrators who toss their manuscripts overboard and go down with the ship.
3. G. R. Thompson, *Poe's Fiction: Romantic Irony in the Gothic Tales*, chapter 1, 3–18.
4. Irwin, *American Hieroglyphics*, 234. Irwin describes this sense of misgiving in trying to ascribe meaning to Tekeli-li: "Yet if, in that ceaseless pursuit

of meaning that characterizes human behavior, we interpret the resemblance between *tkl* and Tekeli-li as the author's intention and are left with the uneasy feeling that we have gone too far, that we have exceeded the limit of what can be known from the evidence, then perhaps we have been made to act out the deepest significance of *Pym*'s ending—the indeterminate status of any interpretation of nature's script, of any reading that discovers the world's meaning, the existence of its Author or His intentions. Such an interpretation may simply be a self-projection that creates the illusion of depth, a shadow mistaken for a body. It is precisely this uncertainty between body and shadow that the ending of *Pym* poses and refuses to solve." I would only point out that the problem posed by the much-disputed ending occurs from the beginning and at every level of the text.

5. Richard Wilbur, Introduction, *The Narrative of Arthur Gordon Pym* (Boston: David R. Godine, 1973), x–xi.

6. Patrick Quinn, *The French Face of Edgar Poe*, 16.

7. Poe, *Complete Works*, 14:199.

8. Kent Ljungquist, "The Descent of the Titans: The Sublime Riddle of *Arthur Gordon Pym*." Ljungquist's fine article discusses this state of mind and the subsequent overstraining of the faculties in terms of Pym's experience but does not relate it to the reader's experience. I think ultimately he identifies the sublime too exclusively with the state of expansion and not with the movement between the two states of mind.

9. Roger Shattuck, *The Banquet Years*, 34.

10. Ibid.

11. Daniel Hoffman, "Disentanglements," *Poe, Poe, Poe, Poe . . .* , 105–36, especially 123–24.

12. D. H. Lawrence, "Edgar Allan Poe," in *Studies in Classic American Literature*, 64.

13. Ibid., 70.

14. Arthur Hobson Quinn, *Edgar Allan Poe: A Critical Biography*, 267.

15. For a somewhat different view of perversity as a moral principle, see Victor Vitanza's "Edgar Allan Poe's *The Narrative of Arthur Gordon Pym:* An Anatomy of Perverseness."

16. Poe, *Complete Works*, 4:146.

17. Ibid., 6:148–50.

18. Ibid., 2:153.

19. Thompson, *Poe's Fiction*, 176.

20. Poe, *Complete Works*, 16:211.

21. Ibid., 11.

22. Ibid.

23. Quinn, *The French Face of Edgar Poe*, 52.

24. Poe, *Complete Works*, 5:88.

25. Poe, *The Narrative of Arthur Gordon Pym*, *Complete Works*, 3:30. All further references to *Pym* will be placed in the text, with pages always referring to volume 3 of the *Works*.

26. James M. Cox, "Edgar Poe: Style as Pose," 77.

27. Poe, *Complete Works*, 8:170.

28. Once the separation of the two voices is recognized, it becomes apparent that Pym does not, as Leonard Engel and others have argued, give any evidence of spiritual growth in the course of the narrative. The growth is the reader's. As Barton Levi St. Armand says, "Pym endures rather than prevails." See their articles in *The American Transcendental Quarterly* 37 (Winter 1978), which is devoted entirely to *Pym*.

29. David Ketterer's "Devious Voyage: *The Singular Narrative of Arthur Gordon Pym*" provides an interesting contrast to my treatment of the structural outlines in *Pym*. Because I emphasize the differences between the two halves of the book, I view with some skepticism his argument that "an acute reader is provided with all the material necessary to construct a Chapter XXVI which echoes Chapter I."

30. T. S. Eliot, "From Poe to Valéry," 219.

31. Poe, *Complete Works*, 6:175.

32. E. H. Davidson, *Poe: A Critical Study*.

33. Sidney Moss, "*Arthur Gordon Pym*, or The Fallacy of Thematic Interpretation," 305. "And in Poe's case we have Davidson's full scale study that demonstrates that all of Poe's themes are reducible to two—a questioning self that would pierce the pasteboard mask of appearances and thereby apprehend ultimate reality, and a solipsistic self that would make 'reality what the inner will ordains.' "

34. Ibid.

35. My conclusions touch on the question of Poe's relationship to or place in the transcendental movement. As is implied by my final comments, I believe that Poe was the transcendentalist par excellence because he embraced its doctrine with a full understanding of its moral implications. The quotations that begin the chapter reflect my belief that Poe was also the sternest moralist of that tradition. If his was "the half-closed eye" that David Ketterer suggests, his was also an unblinking eye. For a further discussion of this relationship, see David Ketterer, *The Rationale of Deception in Poe*, 43–45; Ottavio M. Casale, "Edgar Allan Poe and Transcendentalism: Conflict and Affinity" (Ph.D. diss., University of Michigan, 1965); Ottavio M. Casale, "Poe on Transcendentalism," *Emerson Society Quarterly*, no. 50 (1968): 85–97; Killis Campbell, *The Mind of Poe and Other Studies* (1933; reprint, New York: Russell & Russell, 1962), 14–15; Arnold Smithline, "Eureka: Poe as Transcendentalist," *Emerson Society Quarterly*, no. 39 (1965): 28.

Notes to Chapter II

1. Quoted in Leon Edel, *Henry James: The Master, 1910–1916*, 5:125.

2. J. A. Ward, "The Ineffectual Heroes of James's Middle Period," 315–27.

3. Arnold P. Hinchcliffe, "Henry James's *The Sacred Fount*," 92.

4. Ibid., 93.

5. R. P. Blackmur, "The Sacred Fount," 332.

6. Charles B. Feidelson, Jr., *Symbolism and American Literature*, 26.

7. Ibid., 73.

8. James in an unpublished letter to Mrs. Humphrey Ward, dated 15 March 1901. Quoted in Jean Frantz Blackall, *Jamesian Ambiguity and "The Sacred Fount,"* 144–45.

9. Henry James, *The Letters of Henry James*, 1:408.

10. Leon Edel, Introduction to *The Sacred Fount*, 9.

11. Ibid., 7.

12. Theodore Parker, *Experience as a Minister*, 44.

13. Theodore Parker, "Transcendentalism," in *Theodore Parker: American Transcendentalist*, 65.

14. Henry James, *The Sacred Fount*, 20. Subsequent references to this work are to this edition and will appear in the text.

15. Parker, "Transcendentalism," 69–70.
16. D. W. Jefferson, *Henry James and the Modern Reader,* 179.
17. Jean Frantz Blackall, "The Exclusive Wagnerite," in *Jamesian Ambiguity,* 90–123.
18. Lew Vanderpoole, "Ludwig of Bavaria: A Personal Reminiscence," 536–38.
19. Quoted by Edel, Introduction to *The Sacred Fount,* 5.
20. Blackall, *Jamesian Ambiguity,* 21.
21. James K. Folsom, "Archimago's Well: An Interpretation of *The Sacred Fount,*" 140.
22. William Dean Howells, "Mr. Henry James's Later Work," 135–36.
23. Edel, Introduction to *The Sacred Fount,* 15.
24. Howells, "James's Later Work," 134.
25. Raymond Immerwahr, "Romantic Irony and Romantic Arabesque Prior to Romanticism," 683.
26. Robert J. Andreach, "Henry James's *The Sacred Fount:* The Existential Predicament," *Nineteenth Century Fiction* 17 (December 1962): 197–216.
27. Folsom, "Archimago's Well," 143.
28. Ibid., 139–40.
29. Howells, "James's Later Work," 135.
30. Theodore Parker, "The Writings of Emerson," in *Theodore Parker: American Transcendentalist,* 195.
31. Ibid., 191.
32. Edgar Allan Poe, *Complete Works,* 3:325.
33. Gertrude Stein, *Lectures in America,* 201.
34. Jonathan Culler, *Structuralist Poetics: Structuralism, Linguistics, and the Study of Literature,* 200–201. Culler characterizes the literary convention of limited point of view, used by James and those who followed his lead, as "a last-ditch strategy for humanizing writing and making personality the focal point of the text."
35. James, *Letters,* 1:356.

Notes to Chapter III

1. "P.'s Correspondence," *The Centenary Edition of the Works of Nathaniel Hawthorne,* 10:362. All subsequent references to Hawthorne's writings will be to this edition.
2. "The Custom-House," *The Scarlet Letter,* 1:3.
3. Ibid., 5.
4. Ibid., 35.
5. Ibid., 33–34.
6. James Russell Lowell, "*The Marble Faun:* A Romance of Monte Beni," 2.
7. Theodore Parker, quoted in Austin Warren, Introduction, *Nathaniel Hawthorne: American Writers Series,* lxxi.
8. E. P. Whipple, ibid. Italics mine.
9. Preface, *Twice-Told Tales,* 9:7.
10. Herman Melville, "Hawthorne and His Mosses," in *The Portable Melville,* 406.
11. Charles B. Feidelson, Jr., *Symbolism and American Literature,* 4.
12. Ibid., 7.

13. John Caldwell Stubbs, *The Pursuit of Form: A Study of Hawthorne and the Romance*, xi.
14. Edgar A. Dryden, *Nathaniel Hawthorne: The Poetics of Enchantment*, 11.
15. Kenneth Dauber, *Rediscovering Hawthorne*, 10, 11.
16. Ibid., 203.
17. James K. Folsom, *Man's Accidents and God's Purposes*, 20.
18. F. O. Matthiessen, *American Renaissance*, 350.
19. Stubbs, *The Pursuit of Form*, 46, 47. Discussing Hawthorne's manipulation of his reader in the depiction of Judge Pyncheon's death, Stubbs concludes, "In Hawthorne's four long works we can find a growing emphasis on self-conscious artifice and on the desire to involve the reader in the working out of the writer's inquiry."
20. Postscript, *The Marble Faun*, 4:463–67. References to *The Marble Faun* will hereafter appear in the text.
21. Darrel Abel, "A Masque of Love and Death," 22–23.
22. *The Italian Notebooks*, unavailable in the Ohio edition. References here are to *The Works of Nathaniel Hawthorne*, ed. George Parsons Lathrop, Riverside Edition (Boston: Houghton, Mifflin, and Co., 1883), 10:332.
23. Matthiessen, *American Renaissance*, 280.
24. E. P. Whipple, "Review," in *Merrill Studies in "The Marble Faun,"* 6.
25. It is interesting to compare Hawthorne's use of sculptures possessing motion-in-stillness with T. E. Hulme's appeal to abstract art as presupposing an absolute beyond man and the physical world. See Charles Feidelson's discussion of Hulme, *Symbolism and American Literature*, 214, 215.
26. Feidelson, *Symbolism and American Literature*, 15. Michael Davitt Bell, in *The Development of American Romance*, 134, argues as I will in the ensuing pages, that it is Hawthorne's characters and not Hawthorne himself who are the allegorists: "His plots are not didactically generated by his efforts to tell us what his symbols mean, what abstract notions they picture forth; they grow instead out of his characters' efforts to find out what the symbols mean or at all events to make them mean something. It is these characters who are in intention, the allegorists. Moreover, their allegorical tendency almost always leads to a distortion of life, a refusal to face it directly in its full complexity. Hawthorne thus apparently adopts the allegorical mode in order to turn it against allegorical intentions."
27. *The Italian Notebooks, The Works of Nathaniel Hawthorne*, 10:98.
28. "Main Street," 11:52.
29. Roy Harvey Pearce, "Hawthorne and the Twilight of Romance," 503. Pearce's summary of Hawthorne's use of the sketch follows.
30. Ibid., 500–501.
31. Ibid., 503.
32. Millicent Bell, *Hawthorne's View of the Artist*, 42. Italics mine.
33. Paul Tillich, *A History of Christian Thought: From Its Judaic and Hellenistic Origins to Existentialism*, 124.
34. "The Custom-House," 1:10.
35. Ibid., 9.
36. Ibid., 10.
37. "The Birthmark," 10:304.
38. William James, *The Varieties of Religious Experience*, 77.
39. Ibid., 77–78.
40. *Our Old Home*, 5:261.
41. Ibid., 151–52.

42. *Letters of Hawthorne to William D. Ticknor: 1851–1864*, 99–100.
43. Letter quoted in James T. Fields, *Yesterdays with Authors*, 55–56.
44. Ibid., 89.
45. Ibid., 87.
46. Henry James, *Hawthorne*, 134.
47. Quoted in Warren, *Nathaniel Hawthorne*, xxxiii–xxxiv.
48. Fields, *Yesterdays with Authors*, 103.
49. E. H. Davidson, *Hawthorne's Last Phase*, 112.
50. C. F. Hoffman, quoted in Bertha Faust, *Hawthorne's Contemporaneous Reputation*, 30–31.
51. E. H. Davidson, ed., *Hawthorne's Dr. Grimshawe's Secret*, 105.

Bibliography

Abel, Darrel. "A Masque of Love and Death." *University of Toronto Quarterly* 33 (October 1953): 9–25.

American Transcendental Quarterly 37 (Winter 1978).

Bell, Michael Davitt. *The Development of American Romance: The Sacrifice of Relation.* Chicago: University of Chicago Press, 1980.

Bell, Millicent. *Hawthorne's View of the Artist.* New York: State University of New York, University Publishers, 1962.

Blackall, Jean Frantz. *Jamesian Ambiguity and "The Sacred Fount."* Ithaca: Cornell University Press, 1965.

Blackmur, R. P. "The Sacred Fount." *Kenyon Review* 4 (Autumn 1942): 328–52.

Brodhead, Richard H. *Hawthorne, Melville, and the Novel.* Chicago: University of Chicago Press, 1973.

Buitenhaus, Peter. "Henry James on Hawthorne." *The New England Quarterly* 32 (June 1959): 207–25.

Carlson, Eric W., ed. *The Recognition of Edgar Allan Poe: Selected Criticism Since 1829.* Ann Arbor: University of Michigan Press, 1966.

Cohen, Bernard B. *The Recognition of Nathaniel Hawthorne.* Ann Arbor: University of Michigan Press, 1969.

Cox, James M. "Edgar Poe: Style as Pose." *Virginia Quarterly Review* 44 (Winter 1968): 67–89.

Culler, Jonathan. *Structuralist Poetics: Structuralism, Linguistics, and the Study of Literature.* London: Routledge and Kegan Paul, 1975.

Davidson, E. H. *Hawthorne's Last Phase.* 2d ed. Hamden, Conn.: Archon Books, 1967.

———. *Poe, A Critical Study.* Cambridge: Harvard University Press, 1957.

———, ed. *Hawthorne's Dr. Grimshawe's Secret.* Cambridge: Harvard University Press, 1954.

Dauber, Kenneth. *Rediscovering Hawthorne.* Princeton, N.J.: Princeton University Press, 1977.

Dryden, Edgar A. *Nathaniel Hawthorne: The Poetics of Enchantment.* Ithaca, N.Y.: Cornell University Press, 1977.

Edel, Leon. *Henry James: The Master, 1910–1916.* New York: J. B. Lippincott, 1972.

———. Introduction. *The Sacred Fount.* London: Rupert Hart-Davis, 1959.

Eliot, T. S. "From Poe to Valéry." Library of Congress Lecture, 19 November 1948. *Hudson Review* (Autumn 1949). In *The Recognition of Edgar Allan Poe: Selected Criticism Since 1829,* edited by Eric W. Carlson. Ann Arbor: University of Michigan Press, 1966.

Faust, Bertha. "Hawthorne's Contemporaneous Reputation." Ph.D. diss., University of Pennsylvania, Philadelphia, 1939.
Feidelson, Charles B., Jr. *Symbolism and American Literature.* Chicago: University of Chicago Press, 1953.
Fields, James T. *Yesterdays with Authors.* 1871. Reprint. Cambridge, Mass.: The Riverside Press, 1901.
Folsom, James K. "Archimago's Well: An Interpretation of *The Sacred Fount.*" *Modern Fiction Studies* 7 (Summer 1961): 136–44.
———. *Man's Accidents and God's Purposes.* New Haven, Conn.: College and University Press, 1963.
Frye, Northrop. *The Anatomy of Criticism: Four Essays.* Princeton, N.J.: Princeton University Press, 1957.
Halliburton, David. *Edgar Allan Poe: A Phenomenological View.* Princeton, N.J.: Princeton University Press, 1973.
Hauck, Richard B. *A Cheerful Nihilism: Confidence and "The Absurd" in American Humorous Fiction.* Bloomington: Indiana University Press, 1971.
Hawthorne, Nathaniel. *The Centenary Edition of the Works of Nathaniel Hawthorne.* Edited by William Charvat, Roy Harvey Pearce, Claude M. Simpson, Vols. 1–10. Columbus: Ohio State University Press, 1974.
———. *Letters of Hawthorne to William D. Ticknor: 1851–1864.* Foreword by C. E. Frazer Clark, Jr. 1910. Reprint. Washington, D.C.: NCR Microcard Editions, 1972.
Hinchcliffe, Arnold P. "Henry James's *The Sacred Fount.*" *Texas Studies in Literature and Language* 2 (Spring 1960): 88–94.
Hoffman, Daniel. *Poe, Poe, Poe, Poe . . . .* Garden City, N.Y.: Doubleday and Co., 1972.
Howells, William Dean. "Mr. Henry James's Later Work." *North American Review* 176 (January 1903): 125–37.
Hyslop, Lois, and Francis E. Hyslop, eds. *Baudelaire on Poe.* State College, Penn.: Bald Eagle Press, 1952.
Immerwahr, Raymond. "Romantic Irony and Romantic Arabesque Prior to Romanticism." *German Quarterly* 42 (November 1969): 665–85.
Irwin, John T. *American Hieroglyphics: The Symbol of the Egyptian Hieroglyphics in the American Renaissance.* New Haven, Conn.: Yale University Press, 1980.
Iser, Wolfgang. *The Implied Reader: Patterns of Communication in Prose Fiction from Bunyan to Beckett.* Baltimore: The Johns Hopkins University Press, 1974.
James, Henry. *Hawthorne.* 1880. Reprint. Ithaca, N.Y.: Cornell University Press, 1956.
———. *The Letters of Henry James.* Edited by Percy Lubbock. 2 vols. New York: Charles Scribner's Sons, 1920.
———. *The Sacred Fount.* 1901. Reprint. London: Rupert Hart-Davis, 1959.

James, William. *The Varieties of Religious Experience.* New York: Mentor Books, 1958.
Jefferson, D. W. *Henry James and the Modern Reader.* New York: St. Martin's Press, 1964.
Kesterson, David B., ed. *The Merrill Studies in "The Marble Faun."* Columbus, Ohio: Charles E. Merrill Publishing Company, 1971.
Ketterer, David. "Devious Voyage: *The Singular Narrative of Arthur Gordon Pym.*" *American Transcendental Quarterly* 37 (Winter 1978): 21–33.
———. *The Rationale of Deception in Poe.* Baton Rouge: Louisiana State University Press, 1979.
Knights, L. C. "Henry James and The Trapped Spectator." *Explorations.* New York, 1947.
Krook, Dorothea. *The Ordeal of Consciousness in Henry James.* Cambridge: Cambridge University Press, 1962.
Krutch, Joseph Wood. *Edgar Allan Poe: A Study in Genius.* New York: Russell & Russell, 1965.
Lawrence, D. H. *Studies in Classic American Literature.* London: William Heinemann, 1924.
Liebman, Sheldon W. "The Design of *The Marble Faun.*" In *The Merrill Studies in "The Marble Faun,"* edited by David B. Kesterson. Columbus, Ohio: Charles E. Merrill Publishing Company, 1971.
Ljungquist, Kent. "Descent of the Titans: The Sublime Riddle of *Arthur Gordon Pym.*" *The Southern Literary Journal* 10, no. 2 (Spring 1978): 75–92.
Lowell, James Russell. "*The Marble Faun:* A Romance of Monte Beni." In *The Merrill Studies in "The Marble Faun,"* edited by David B. Kesterson. Columbus, Ohio: Charles E. Merrill Publishing Company, 1971.
Lundblad, Jane. *Nathaniel Hawthorne and the Tradition of Gothic Romance.* Cambridge: Harvard University Press, 1946.
Lynen, John F. *The Design of the Present: Essays on Time and Form in American Literature.* New Haven, Conn.: Yale University Press, 1969.
Male, Roy R. *Hawthorne's Tragic Vision.* New York: W. W. Norton and Company, 1964.
———. "The Transfiguration of Figures: *The Marble Faun.*" In *The Merrill Studies in "The Marble Faun,"* edited by David B. Kesterson. Columbus, Ohio: Charles E. Merrill Publishing Company, 1971.
Matthiessen, F. O. *American Renaissance.* New York: Oxford University Press, 1968.
Melville, Herman. *The Portable Melville.* Edited by Jay Leyda. New York: The Viking Press, 1952.
Moss, Sydney. "*Arthur Gordon Pym,* or The Fallacy of Thematic Interpretation." *New Letters* 33 (June 1967): 299–306.
Parker, Theodore. *Experience as a Minister with Some Account of His Early Life and Education for the Ministry.* Boston: Rufus Leighton, Jr., 1859.

———. *Theodore Parker: American Transcendentalist*. Edited by Robert E. Collins. Metuchen, N.J.: The Scarecrow Press, 1973.

Pearce, Roy Harvey. "Hawthorne and The Twilight of Romance." *Yale Review* 37 (March 1948): 487–506.

Poe, Edgar Allan. *The Complete Works of Edgar Allan Poe, Marginalia—Eureka*. 17 vols. Edited by James A. Harrison. 1902. Reprint. New York: AMS Press, 1965.

Quinn, Arthur Hobson. *Edgar Allan Poe: A Critical Biography*. New York: D. Appleton-Century Company, 1941.

Quinn, Patrick. *The French Face of Edgar Poe*. Carbondale: Southern Illinois University Press, 1957.

Rowe, John C. "The Authority of the Sign in Henry James's *The Sacred Fount*." *Criticism* 19 (Summer 1977): 223–40.

Scholes, Robert. *Structuralism in Literature: An Introduction*. New Haven, Conn.: Yale University Press, 1974.

Shattuck, Roger. *The Banquet Years*. 2d ed. New York: Vintage-Knopf, 1968.

Spencer, Sharon. *Space, Time and Structure in the Modern Novel*. Chicago: The Swallow Press, 1971.

Stein, Gertrude. *Lectures in America*. New York: Random House, 1935.

Stein, William Bysshe. *Hawthorne's Faust: A Study of the Devil Archetype*. 1953. Reprint. Hamden, Conn.: Archon Books, 1968.

Stubbs, John Caldwell. *The Pursuit of Form: A Study of Hawthorne and the Romance*. Urbana: University of Illinois Press, 1970.

Tanner, Tony. *City of Words: American Fiction 1950–1970*. New York: Harper and Row, 1971.

Tate, Allan. *Collected Essays*. Denver: Alan Swallow, 1959.

Thompson, G. R. *Poe's Fiction: Romantic Irony in the Gothic Tales*. Madison: University of Wisconsin Press, 1973.

Tillich, Paul. *A History of Christian Thought: From Its Judaic and Hellenistic Origins to Existentialism*. Edited by Carl E. Braaten. New York: Touchstone-Simon and Schuster, 1967.

Tompkins, Jane P., ed. *Reader-Response Criticism: From Formalism to Post-Structuralism*. Baltimore: The Johns Hopkins University Press, 1980.

Vanderpoole, Lew. "Ludwig of Bavaria: A Personal Reminiscence." *Lippincott's Monthly Magazine* 38 (November 1886): 535–39.

Vitanza, Victor. "Edgar Allan Poe's *The Narrative of Arthur Gordon Pym:* An Anatomy of Perverseness." *Etudes Anglaises* 27 (March 1974): 26–37.

Von Abele, Rudolf. *The Death of the Artist*. The Hague: Martinus Nijhoff, 1955.

Ward, J. A. "The Ineffectual Heroes of James's Middle Period." *Texas Studies in Literature and Language* 2 (Autumn 1960): 315–27.

Warren, Austin. Introduction. *Nathaniel Hawthorne: American Writers Series*. Chicago: American Book Company, 1934.

Index